The
Ikaria Way

ALSO BY DIANE KOCHILAS

My Greek Table:
Authentic Flavors and Modern Home Cooking
from My Kitchen to Yours

The Greek Vegetarian:
More Than 100 Recipes Inspired by the
Traditional Dishes and Flavors of Greece

The Food and Wine of Greece:
More Than 250 Classic and Modern Dishes
from the Mainland and Islands of Greece

The
Ikaria Way

100 DELICIOUS PLANT-BASED RECIPES INSPIRED BY MY HOMELAND,
THE GREEK ISLAND OF LONGEVITY

Diane Kochilas

ST. MARTIN'S GRIFFIN
NEW YORK

First published in the United States by St. Martin's Griffin, an imprint of St. Martin's Publishing Group

THE IKARIA WAY. Copyright © 2024 by Diane Kochilas. All rights reserved. Printed in China. For information, address St. Martin's Publishing Group, 120 Broadway, New York, NY 10271.

www.stmartins.com

Endpaper photograph and photographs on pp. ii–iii, viii–1, 14, 25, 26–27, 32, 42, 50–51, 90–91, 102, 106, 122–23, 156–57, 186–87, 202, 214, 222, 230, 237, 238–39, 250–51, and 254 by Shutterstock.com

All other photography by Vasilis Stenos

Designed by Jan Derevjanik

The Library of Congress Cataloging-in-Publication Data is available upon request.

ISBN 978-1-250-88000-0 (paper over board)
ISBN 978-1-250-88001-7 (ebook)

Our books may be purchased in bulk for promotional, educational, or business use. Please contact your local bookseller or the Macmillan Corporate and Premium Sales Department at 1-800-221-7945, extension 5442, or by email at MacmillanSpecialMarkets@macmillan.com.

First Edition: 2024

10 9 8 7 6 5 4 3 2 1

For Kyveli and Yiorgo.
And . . . in loving memory of my beautiful kitchen companion,
Jazzy, who even liked plants, and of JN, who helped me
hash out this book and left way too early.

contents

The
Ikaria Way

introduction

The Ikaria Way was born in the summer of 2021 on Ikaria, the Blue-Zone Greek island where "people forget to die," as the venerable *New York Times* wrote a few years ago. I have deep family roots on the island, and for almost two decades, I have been running a cooking school out of the kitchen and garden of my village home. It was at one such weeklong class that the idea for this book was sparked. I had two guests from Montana who stood in bewilderment at the kitchen counter on the third day of the class and confessed that they not only ate meat three times a day back home, but they also never imagined that plant-based cooking, which is mostly—but not all of—what we do during our week together on the island, could be so satisfying, varied, and real.

It was a eureka moment for me. What I take naturally to be the "right" way to eat, mostly plant-based meals, with occasional (totally guilt-free) diversions that sometimes include a little meat, fish, or dairy, was to them an absolute revelation. Granted, having a garden and an island with incredibly varied and rich flora at my fingertips makes cooking and teaching about plant-based foods easy. But this book aims to make the lessons of Ikaria accessible to modern cooks anywhere, using ingredients that are readily available in most shops and markets.

I am not a vegan. I just eat a diet of real food grown locally with an overwhelming amount of vegetables, greens, beans, great Greek olive oil, herbs, spices, whole grains, crunchy sea salt, and all the other gifts of the earth with which we happen to be blessed in the Mediterranean. The "grown locally" is important; one can adopt the Mediterranean diet and the old Ikarian way of eating a mostly green diet regardless of where one lives. I do love cheese and honey, and as a cook with Greek roots, it would be not only difficult but most unpleasant to live—or cook—without them, so most of the guilty pleasures in these pages are meltingly good thanks to a little cheese!

The Ikaria Way aims to bring the spirit of the island and its plant-based traditions to a wider audience. Ikaria is a Blue Zone, a term coined more than a decade ago by Dan Buettner and his team of researchers, who were studying longevity patterns around the world. They discovered this remote island to be one of a handful of places around the globe where people live an inordinately long time. The term was coined when one of the team members literally circled these places on a map in blue pen!

In 2009, a group of Greek physicians and researchers conducted the Ikaria Study, corroborating what Buettner and his team had surmised. The Athens Medical School team looked at the local diet, lifestyle, and income levels of a sample population of 1,420 Ikarians. (The island's total permanent population is about eight thousand.) They discovered that 13 percent of the study's sample subjects had a life expectancy over the age of eighty. Globally, the over-eighty age group accounts for just 1 percent of the population; in North America and Europe, the octogenarians and over make up 3 percent of the population. Another peculiarity of Ikaria is that men and women both seem to age equally well. In most of the rest of the world, men tend to die before their partners. Another startling revelation is that Ikarians are ten times more likely to live to one hundred than Americans.

I spend almost half the year on the island and cook very locally when I am there. But I also came to see that I carried the lessons of Ikaria wherever I go, by trying to live a calm life, not stressing out about much, and embracing local ingredients wherever I am. So, in creating the recipes for this book, I venture beyond the local larder but stay true to a spirit of cooking that is simple, vibrant, and rooted in the tenets of the greater Mediterranean diet. Tofu is an example of food that is not traditional to Greece. I've come to embrace it and adapt it to my way of cooking, with olive oil, fresh seasonal vegetables, and herbs. In this age of global accessibility, tofu is actually even available, up there with chia seeds, quinoa, and goji berries, in a few of the markets on the island. My goal is to provide a template for cooking like an Ikarian in a global world.

In my life and kitchen, I try really hard to stay away from processed foods, and I am philosophically perplexed by the whole notion of vegan meat and starch-packed vegan cheese. I avoid plant-based imitations of animal foods, except for a few recipes in which I suggest cashew milk. Of all the vegan cheeses out there, I have found the cashew-milk cheeses to be the closest approximation of real cheese; as for the plant-based milks, my kids showed me the way, having gone off cow's milk for a few years now.

We live in crazy dietary times. In my experience as a cook and cooking teacher, I never cease to be amazed by two things: how extreme people's neuroses about food and eating have become and how little most people actually know about cooking and eating well. This book is my response to those two issues: how to be good to your body without being mean to your mind, and how to cook in the spirit of a relaxed, healing kind of island where the tempo of life is slow and easy and where people connect through food around a table. Cooking shouldn't be another stressful moment in our day!

My background as a Greek-Mediterranean cook is steeped in the deep traditions of plant-based cuisine that has evolved over centuries. Greeks are, indeed, almost vegan, but they'd never call themselves that. The array of plant-based (main course) dishes in the Greek diet is unsurpassed anywhere else in the Mediterranean, and they developed because poverty forbade anything resembling a frequent indulgence in animal products, as did religion. Many Greeks still fast for half the year, as the religious calendar dictates, thereby foregoing most animal products during those periods.

On a personal level, my DNA as a daughter of Ikaria has blessed me with a naturally relaxed attitude toward most things in life, especially food. Indeed "relax" is the keyword in my whole approach to cooking and eating. Food equals pleasure, and cooking is the vehicle for delivering that. In the spirit of Ikaria, that means sharing a plate or two with friends, drinking some wine, creating a ritual around the table that involves simply sitting down, taking a breath, and respecting the meal in front of us enough to put away our gadgets and focus on what we're eating.

In this collection of plant-based recipes, I am offering people a way to reconcile the extremes, the divisiveness and fear that we have allowed—yes, it's our choice—to pervade every part of our modern lives. The recipes are a mix of traditional and contemporary dishes. They aim to be simple, almost entirely plant-based with some cheese here and there, prepared with real food and almost nothing processed save for the occasional can of tomatoes. My pantry, and the one I will suggest for readers, is culled from the traditions of the Mediterranean: chock-full of all the things that have long given food its flavor in this part of the world: herbs, olives, nuts, and more. The dishes have to have "craveability," which is born when textures, robust flavors, and mouthfeel, achieved with the inclusion of good fats like olive oil, work harmoniously together. I made a conscious decision not to include dessert recipes. As

for during our Ikaria classes, mostly what we serve after a meal is fresh, seasonal fruit, which is the real tradition on the island.

Food is about nourishment of body, mind, and spirit. It's about pleasure and giving and should not be a source of stress or guilt. *The Ikaria Way* is a loose and loving road map for how to make and enjoy food that happens to be almost all plant-based and always natural, but with a little wiggle room.

The Ikaria way is essentially the Mediterranean diet coupled with the fresh, seasonal local ingredients we can find wherever we live. It's less a diet with all the strict rules and dos and don'ts of what you can and cannot eat, and more a mindset. A basic road map, as I like to call it. Food should equal pleasure! The Mediterranean diet should be accessible anywhere. It's just a matter of knowing what elements, techniques, and Mediterranean ingredients are the most important.

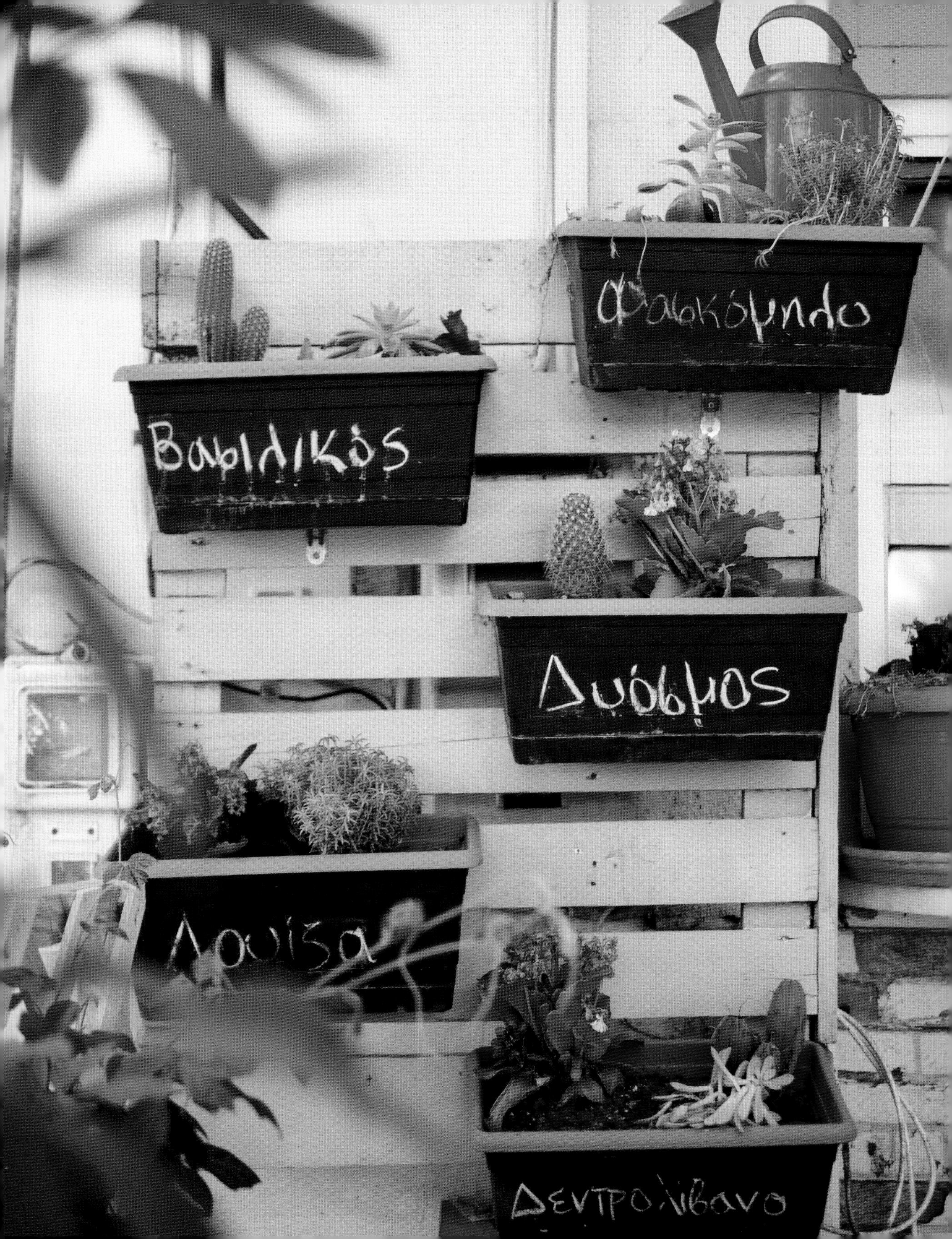
Φασκόμηλο
Βασιλικός
Δυόσμος
Λουίζα
Δεντρολίβανο

a pantry inspired by ikaria

Beans and Legumes

Among the seminal ingredients of the Ikarian way of eating are beans and pulses. These varied and versatile pantry items pack a nutritional punch. Beans and pulses are one of the oldest foods consumed in Greece, a staple that provides a simple, healthy, and inexpensive way to care for your body. Greeks consume many different kinds of beans and pulses, and among the oldest are the broad bean, the chickpea, and the lentil, which are some of the earliest cultivated beans and legumes.

Adding beans and pulses to your everyday meal plan is proven to increase longevity. Simple changes like eating at least three servings of beans each week will also help you to phase meat out of your diet. You can even pair these with a grain like barley or quinoa to help you hit your dietary goals. Below is a list of some of the main beans and pulses consumed in Greece and in Ikaria, all widely available.

BROAD BEANS OR FAVA BEANS

One of the oldest traditional beans cultivated in the Eastern Mediterranean, broad beans, aka fava beans, have a complex history. They're exceedingly nutritious on the one hand, but on the other, they can be dangerous for anyone lacking the enzyme needed to digest them.

On the nutrition front, there's a literal laundry list of body parts that benefit by the consumption of broad beans. Broad beans are rich in protein, fiber, vitamins (especially vitamin C), minerals (a good source of manganese and iron), and the amino acid L-DOPA, which helps in the production of dopamine, the neurotransmitters that keep our central nervous system running properly and the lack of which is associated with Parkinson's disease. Eyes, teeth, bones, and brain all benefit from broad bean consumption. These ancient beans, cultivated for more than six thousand years in the Mediterranean, also work to prevent cancer, anemia, osteoporosis, and stroke. We sleep better when we eat them, too. On the flip side, though, they can be detrimental to people lacking G6PD, the enzyme that helps red blood cells work properly. For people lacking this enzyme, the consumption of broad beans causes a type of anemia in which red blood cells break down faster than they are produced.

CHICKPEAS

Chickpeas are another of the very ancient staples in the Greek kitchen, and there are many ways to cook them. They're another good replacement for meat, with plenty of protein, but they are also a great source of vitamins, minerals, and fiber, while also helping with managing your weight, helping out with digestion, and reducing the risk of heart disease.

GIGANTES

Gigantes, or giant beans, are one of the most iconic Greek ingredients. They are loaded with protein, making them the perfect protagonist in main course recipes like the Caramelized Giant Beans with Turmeric,

TOFU

I never thought I'd see the day when I'd be touting the virtues of the ultimate Asian ingredient in a book of plant-based Mediterranean diet recipes inspired by the foodways of happy-go-lucky Greek islanders. But here I am doing just that, thanks in part to Dan Buettner, creator of the term Blue Zones, whose short videos about the foods embraced by long-living peoples have inspired me to adapt tofu to my Greek and Mediterranean recipes. I am forever won over.

Tofu—bean curd—is produced by curdling soy milk and pressing it into solid blocks. It comes in numerous textures, from soft and silky, to firm and solid, almost like the consistency of feta cheese. It's a very ancient food; the Japanese have been making it for more than two thousand years.

Soy has a mixed reputation. It is one of the most prevalent GMO (genetically modified organism) plants on the planet, and it also contains an amino acid called tyramine, which helps regulate our blood pressure—although it breaks down if you're on medication for mood disorders or Parkinson's disease. Always opt for organic tofu and avoid tofu altogether if you take medicines called MAOIs (monoamine oxidase inhibitors). There have also been concerns about tofu and increased estrogen levels that may cause breast cancer, but these have been disproven.

Tofu is mostly associated with great nutrition and health-giving properties. It is one of the best sources of plant-based protein there is, and unlike other plant proteins, tofu contains all nine essential amino acids, which our bodies cannot produce on their own. Three ounces of tofu will keep you full for hours.

Tofu is also full of vitamins and minerals and is a good source of iron, potassium, manganese, selenium, phosphorus, magnesium, copper, zinc, and vitamin B.

Plant estrogens, like those in tofu, help prevent hot flashes, improve heart health by keeping the blood vessels inside our hearts healthy, and keep our bones strong. Tofu is also rich in calcium and vitamin D, which is good for bone health, too. Tofu consumption helps lower bad cholesterol and may help slow the growth of prostate cancer. Some studies also show that it is good for brain health and memory.

In the kitchen, it's a versatile workhorse and chameleon and a great replacement for just about everything from eggs to cheese. I always thought of it as bland until I started to adapt it to the vibrant, robust flavors of the Mediterranean diet, and I now see it as a tabula rasa for just about anything. I mostly use the firmest tofu I can find, always organic, and have sprinkled it throughout the recipes in this book in everything from salads, in lieu of hard-boiled eggs, to vegetarian mains. It's great seared and served with all sorts of savory toppings, from mushrooms to greens.

Fennel & Romaine on page 134. Their heartiness makes them a great replacement for meat; they're also low in saturated fats. You can substitute gigantes with butter beans, as they are quite similar in size and texture.

LENTILS

This humble pulse is a nutritional powerhouse, packed with protein and fiber as well as potassium, iron, and other vitamins. There are many varieties of lentils that are native or popular around the Mediterranean. On Ikaria, you can still find them growing wild, and their ancestor, the common vetch, blankets the island with its tiny purple flowers in the spring. I've come to expand on my lentil love by experimenting with non-Greek but easy-to-find varieties like red lentils (dahl), which cook up fast and easily; see Red Lentil Soup with Ginger, Turmeric & Vegetables on page 96.

SPLIT PEAS

If you're already familiar with Greek meze traditions, you have probably heard of fava, which are yellow split peas in Greece. They're a staple and one of the most ancient foods in the Eastern Mediterranean, cultivated on several Greek islands and important in the local diet everywhere, Ikaria included. The most common way to cook yellow split peas is in an eponymous puree, also referred to as fava, which can be served in many ways, including as a dip, soup, and accompaniment for countless savory toppings or preparations. Over the years, I've included a recipe for fava puree in almost every one of my cookbooks. Here, I marry it with some heirloom carrots (page 31).

Garlic

I couldn't imagine my life or kitchen without garlic! It's the ultimate flavor-packing, health-providing natural ingredient, a virtual pharmacopeia of goodness in every clove. The vast majority of recipes in these pages calls for garlic!

Interest in and knowledge of garlic as a superfood goes back to the beginning of recorded history. Remnants of garlic have been found in Egyptian pyramids and ancient Greek temples, such as Knossos in Crete, which was built between 1400 and 1800 BCE. It seems to always have been considered a strengthening substance. Hippocrates, the father of medicine, prescribed garlic for a whole litany of health conditions, from pulmonary to gynecological. Athletes consumed it to enhance their performance during the ancient Greek Olympics, and it was an important part of the ancient Greek military diet, especially before battle.

Modern-day Ikarians swear by it! My daughter makes a preventative infusion of raw garlic, mountain or sage tea, ginger, and honey, which she consumes when the temperature drops or she feels a cold coming on, advice taken from our friend, Yiorgos Stenos, ninety-one, who once told me that a similar concoction was the panacea of his generation.

Beyond its considerable health-giving properties, one of the reasons why we love garlic so much is that it tastes so good and makes almost everything else taste better, too. Garlic sweetens up as it softens and cooks, lending an almost caramelized flavor to so many different foods. In these pages, you'll find it in just about everything from small plates to sips!

Garlic cheats: I confess to some occasional laziness when it comes to garlic and revert to two Greek products I have found to be time-savers: garlic pureed with olive oil and oregano and whole garlic cloves in brine. The prechopped garlic found in most American supermarkets works for me, too, but it doesn't have anywhere near the complex, rich flavor and aroma as its Greek counterparts.

Grains

Whole grains are an integral part of the Ikaria diet, which is essentially a traditional Mediterranean diet. The regular consumption of whole grains helps reduce our risk of many chronic diseases, including heart disease and stroke. The classic, old island diet was one of whole grains like bulgur or dried corn, both of which people could grow locally, as well as beans, mushrooms, wild greens, garden vegetables, and seasonal fruit. Whole grains are delicious, nutty, filling, packed with nutrients, and very versatile.

Here are a few different types of grains that should be ever-present in the pantry: Bulgur, which is cracked wheat that has been parboiled, takes very little time to cook, and is extremely versatile in everything from salads to soups and stuffings. Farro (or emmer) is an ancient variety of wheat that was domesticated in the Fertile Crescent. A similar ancient wheat in Greece is zea. Both are nutty and pleasantly chewy.

I always have a few boxes of whole wheat pasta varieties on hand for a quick meal, and I have come to love many of the gluten-free bean-based pastas, such as chickpea and lentil pasta. Whole wheat pasta is made with whole wheat flour that contains the bran, hull, and germ of the grain. It has more micronutrients and fiber than regular pasta and a tasty, nutty flavor.

The last few years have seen an explosion of high-protein pasta usually made from chickpea or lentil flour. There is such a wide range out there that it's hard to delineate the best ones. I always look for pasta that has at least 7 grams of protein per serving and as few ingredients as possible, every one of them pronounceable!

Other grains that are useful to have on hand in the pantry include brown rice, various types of white rice (we can indulge on occasion, especially when rice is cooked with vegetables or beans), quinoa, Israeli couscous, and wild rice.

Herbs

DRIED HERBS

Like fresh herbs, dried herbs also make the Mediterranean diet and cooking in the spirit of Ikaria so flavorful. They also play an important role in traditional Greek medicine (see more on the therapeutic use of herbs in the "Sips" chapter, page 240). While fresh herbs add their unique vibrancy to many dishes, dried herbs are also used liberally and are easier to store and make for very basic pantry items. Basic dried herbs include bay leaves, oregano, savory, thyme, and mint.

Bay Leaves
The sprawling bay bush in the front of my Ikarian garden provides endless flavor from its leaves, both fresh and dried. On Ikaria,

bay leaves are added to dried figs to help keep bacteria away and are a staple in most bean soups and stews, making them more palatable and less flatulent. When fresh, they have a flavor that always reminds me of allspice, and when they are dried, that's even more pronounced with hints of bitterness, too.

Oregano

First among equals is definitely Greek oregano. Oregano is one of the defining flavors of Greek cuisine. There are several varieties of wild oregano that grow on Ikaria, and they've been studied for the exceptionally high presence of essential oils, which makes the local varieties potent and extraordinarily aromatic. Indeed, the whole island smells of oregano!

Most Greek oregano is quite aromatic, and I highly recommend it over oregano from other places around the world. It is one of the seminal herbs, and this is a good thing because its high concentration of antioxidants helps fight cellular damage related to many different chronic diseases. Greek oregano is packed with antiviral and antibiotic properties, too, one reason why it has long been consumed as a folk remedy and infusion to combat colds and infections. The best way to take advantage of oregano's health benefits is to use it regularly, so add it liberally to everything from sauces to marinades to dressings!

Savory

Savory is *throumbi* or *thrimvi* in the Ikarian dialect, and it grows wild all over the slopes of Ikaria. It is a favorite herb in all sorts of plant-based and other dishes. It is also consumed as an infusion and is considered helpful for alleviating coughs and arthritis pains and for detoxing.

Thyme

Thyme is another native herb that is rich in antioxidants, and it also has antibiotic properties. Thyme has delicious lemon and floral notes, so it can enhance a range of dishes.

Mint

Mint is one of the herbs used interchangeably in both fresh and dried form, and there are many varieties on the island. One of the most revered locally, pennyroyal, is extremely difficult to find elsewhere. Mint is used to perk up salads and grain and bean dishes and is often paired with greens and other vegetables in savory pies.

FRESH HERBS

One of the things that distinguishes Greek cooking from the cooking in many other parts of the Mediterranean is the profuse use of fresh herbs in so many recipes. The palette of Greek cooking is more herbal than spice-based. Inspired by Ikaria, where myriad herbs grow wild, I use these herbs with abandon in many of my recipes. That's not to say, of course, that we don't use spices—we do, and have a special affinity for warm spices like cinnamon, cloves, nutmeg, and allspice. But the flora brims year-round with herbs, and they play a unique role both in the kitchen and as folk medicine. On Ikaria, most families have a cupboard packed with dried herbs, the therapeutic qualities of which are contained in the knowledge passed down from one generation to the next.

All too often, we use herbs simply as a garnish, missing out on their tremendous health benefits. The use of fresh herbs, with their vibrant and sparkling flavors, helps us to reduce the amount of salt we use. And several herbs, including common parsley, are rich in the essential vitamins A, C, and K.

Herbs are also a great source of protective polyphenols. These are plant compounds with powerful antioxidant, anti-inflammatory, and antibacterial effects, helping to fight a modern laundry list of ailments from cancer to heart disease to diabetes to Alzheimer's disease.

On Ikaria, and in this book inspired by the island's food and lifeways, the robust, natural flavors of herbs are a hallmark of the kitchen. Most of us can grow a few pots of herbs wherever we live, even if it's just on the windowsill, and that's the best way to have ready access to a bevy of aromatic herbs. Growing them ourselves also helps reduce plastic waste since so many herbs come prepackaged in way too much plastic.

Nuts

Nuts are an important ingredient in many of my plant-based recipes and traditionally are an important ingredient in Greek regional cooking in ways that might surprise you. They grow abundantly throughout Greece.

The health benefits of nuts and their place in the Mediterranean diet have long been touted. Their high (good) fat and protein content makes them both satiating and delicious. Nuts are rich in most of the vitamins and minerals our body needs. They're an excellent source of omega-3 fatty acids, a salve for so many ailments, from age-related cognitive disorders like dementia and Alzheimer's disease to rheumatoid arthritis. Nuts are high in fat and low in carbs and are a very good source of several nutrients, including vitamin E, magnesium, and selenium.

I use them to enhance textures in many different dishes, to thicken soups when opting out of dairy—ground, they make an excellent substitute for heavy cream! Indeed, using nuts as a thickener is a very old cooking technique in the Greek kitchen. They're also the ultimate Mediterranean diet snack, offering many benefits and helping to keep us easily sated between meals.

Here are a few of the most popular—and healthiest—nuts and seeds you'll find in Greece.

ALMONDS

Almonds are another ancient favorite. Almonds are good sources of healthy fats, fiber, and protein and are very high in antioxidants, especially their skin. They've been linked to all kinds of health benefits like reduced blood pressure, lower "bad" cholesterol, and even weight loss. They take center stage in quite a few Greek sweets, but for something savory, I like to add them (and pistachios) to recipes like the Grilled Peaches & Arugula Salad with Feta on page 59. Nuts and seeds have been a staple in the Greek diet for ages. They've earned their place by being a versatile, nourishing addition to a wide range of dishes. Make them a part of your daily diet along with other health-promoting habits of the Mediterranean lifestyle.

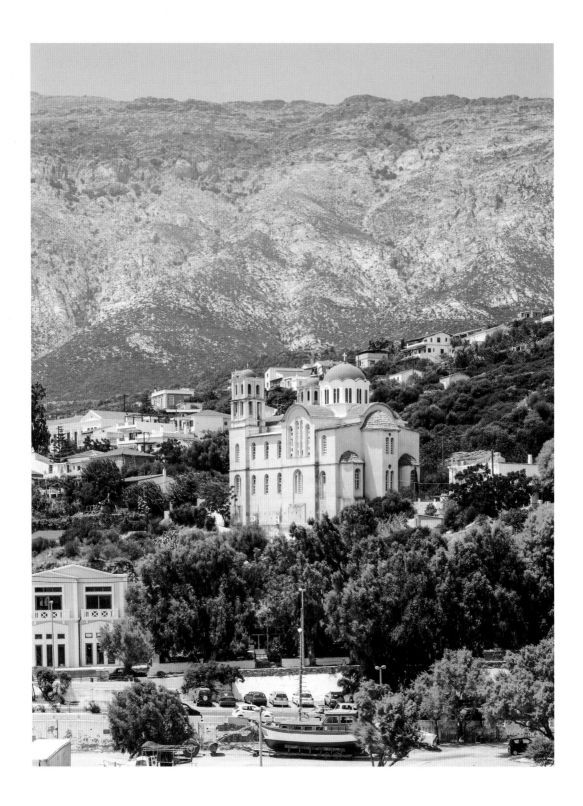

PISTACHIOS

Pistachios have been cultivated in Greece since the beginning of the twentieth century and have flourished so well on the Saronic Gulf island of Aegina that they now have protected designation of origin (PDO) status. Because of the dry climate, Greek pistachios are much smaller than most others cultivated elsewhere and have a more concentrated flavor. Pistachios are one of the healthiest nuts, too. Among the lowest in calories, pistachios contain more antioxidants than almost all other nuts. Antioxidants help to fight all kinds of chronic and age-related diseases, and, interestingly, antioxidants in pistachios are especially digestible, which makes them more easily absorbed into the body.

SESAME SEEDS AND TAHINI

Tahini, a paste made from sesame seeds, is traditionally used during periods of fasting in lieu of olive oil and dairy, as it is one of the most calcium-rich foods on the planet. In the US, tahini is mostly an afterthought—we know it mainly for its use in hummus. But the small sesame seed packs such an amazing nutritional punch that it's worth a starring role on our table.

Staples of the Greek diet abound in antioxidants, and this is especially true for the sesame seed. Antioxidants combat chronic diseases like cancer, diabetes, and heart disease. The sesame seeds that make up tahini contain antioxidant fibers known as lignans. Two lignans in particular, sesamin and sesamol, seem to have the most potent health benefits, and numerous studies have found them to have powerful anticancer properties. The antioxidants in tahini and sesame seeds are so powerful that there is emerging evidence that they may actually be antibacterial! Although scientists are just now uncovering these bacteria-fighting effects, some cultures have long used sesame oil for wound care in patients with diabetes.

The antioxidants in sesame seeds are also highly anti-inflammatory, which is good news since diseases of inflammation seem to be on the rise. While the research is just beginning, animal studies have shown promising evidence that sesamin can be effective in treating inflammatory conditions like asthma, lung disease, and rheumatoid arthritis.

And the health benefits of tahini extend to other chronic diseases. In a clinical trial, patients with type 2 diabetes consumed 2 tablespoons of tahini with their daily breakfast for six weeks while a control group continued their usual diet. At the end of the study, the group that consumed tahini had significantly lower triglyceride levels (a risk factor for cardiovascular disease) compared with those who didn't. Sesame seeds also contain monounsaturated fats, which reduce the risk of type 2 diabetes and cardiovascular disease, and a host of vital nutrients, including protein, fats, carbohydrates, copper, manganese, calcium, phosphorus, magnesium, iron, and many others.

It seems that thousands of years ago, Hippocrates really knew his stuff when he said, "Let food be thy medicine, and medicine be thy food." And luckily for us, eating tahini is much more enjoyable than taking medicine. It's delicious as a simple spread on toast, a dressing on salads or vegetables, and a sauce for pasta. It's also delicious mixed either with Greek honey or *petimezi* (grape molasses)!

PROBIOTICS AND FERMENTED FOODS

Probiotics—the name literally means "for life"—are one of the great longevity food categories of Ikarians and other long-living, healthy people around the world. Probiotics are the strains of good bacteria found in naturally fermented foods such as naturally cured olives (in salt brine), real Greek yogurt, and fermented cheeses—think Greek feta. Probiotic bacteria colonize our gut and keep it healthy, pushing out harmful bacteria that cause inflammation and a host of other ailments.

For the last few summers, I have made batch after batch of probiotic pickled vegetables by putting up the overwhelming amount of cucumbers, green beans, purslane, and peppers that my garden so generously provides in a simple salt brine. That's the key. Vinegar brines kill the probiotics, whereas salt brine enables them to develop. When you make probiotic pickled vegetables at home (I've experimented with beets, carrots, green beans, cucumbers, of course, cabbage, green beans, and peppers), you're basically making a simple salt solution of 2½ tablespoons of sea salt for every quart of water. You can add garlic, spices, and herbs, and it's important to keep whatever it is you're pickling under the surface of the liquid. Sometimes, I add a couple of fresh grape leaves and a rock to hold everything down.

Probiotic pickled vegetables are one of the most common snack foods on Ikaria. Olives, homemade local cheese in salt brine, a kind of primitive goat's milk feta called *kathoura*, fermented cabbage, and brined hyacinth bulbs—what southern Italians also know as *lampascione*—are some of the deliciously sour treats you might encounter around a table in an Ikarian home.

You can opt to experiment, or you can search to find commercially prepared probiotic vegetables. Just be sure the label reads "naturally fermented" and not simply "pickled."

WALNUTS

Walnuts are perhaps one of the most popular nuts in Greek cuisine, and the ancient Greeks believed them to have medicinal properties. They were on to something because walnuts, like pistachios, abound in antioxidants and are one of the best plant sources of omega-3 fatty acids. In Ikaria and generally in Greece, walnuts are commonly paired with honey. When walnuts are paired with garlic, as in the recipe for Smoked Eggplant with Tahini & Walnuts on page 33, we get an immunity-boosting recipe that's also delicious!

Olives

Olives, the ultimate probiotic snack (see page 16), have been a staple in the Greek diet since prehistoric times, and they are one of the many preserves I always keep stocked in my pantry. It's hard to think of a dish that isn't enhanced by the addition of olives. They add a complex flavor and richness to almost anything, and because they're preserved, they can keep indefinitely. In Greece, they are traditionally eaten on their own or added to a salad, but they make a tremendously versatile cooking ingredient. I love to pair them with other pantry staples like beans or pasta and other grains.

Olives, naturally, offer the same amazing health benefits as their derivative, olive oil. They are a good source of iron, calcium, copper, and vitamin E. The calcium in olives has been especially important to Greeks who have traditionally observed 180 days of religious fasting from animal products. In fact, studies have shown that osteoporosis is less common in the Mediterranean than in other parts of Europe primarily because of the high consumption of olives and olive oil.

But what makes olives such a nutritional powerhouse is their abundance of polyphenols. They rank among the fruits (yes, they're fruits!) with the highest concentrations of polyphenols or antioxidant plant compounds. The polyphenols in olives benefit us in two main ways—by reducing both inflammation and oxidative stress (or cellular damage). And these two effects benefit virtually every system in the body. The list of health benefits includes the reduction of cardiac risk factors and inflammation and even fighting cancer! While olives are delicious in their own right, you can't make a better nutritional case for incorporating them into your diet.

There are so many varieties of olives but also various ways of processing them that contribute to their unique flavors and textures. Many Greek olive varieties have PDO status—meaning they're only grown and processed in a particular area of Greece. They truly are a pantry workhorse, adding so much flavor and nutrition to virtually any recipe.

Olive Oil

Olive oil is the defining food of the Mediterranean diet and an absolute must in the pantry. Many of the health benefits associated with the Mediterranean diet, and, by extension, the Ikaria diet, are attributed to the health properties of olive oil.

Greece has been producing olive oil since Minoan times (as early as 3000 BCE!),

THE INCREDIBLE HEALTH BENEFITS OF OLIVE OIL

Let food be thy medicine, and medicine be thy food. **–HIPPOCRATES, 460–375 BCE**

The liberal use of extra-virgin olive oil (EVOO) is key to cooking and eating the Ikarian way. Olive oil can work with the body to fight against many ailments, especially as we age. In Ikaria, it's a salve for many illnesses in the folk pharmacopeia, both ingested and used topically.

Olive oil contains an impressive list of anticancer properties. The various polyphenols found in high-quality extra-virgin olive oil have antitumor and immunomodulator activities. This means that olive oil can bolster the body's anticancer efforts in two general ways: first, by supporting better immune system functioning through an increase in white blood cells (some of which are cancer-killing cells), and second, by directly inhibiting certain cancer cells.

Studies have shown the particular efficacy of these compounds in mitigating the proliferation of specific types of cancer cells; namely, those of malignant mesothelioma and pancreatic, breast, and prostate cancers. The reasons for these effects are multifaceted and complex, but one of the simpler explanations is that the polyphenols in olive oil slow and prevent certain age-related cell behaviors. As many cancers are a result of aging, this prevention of certain aspects of cellular changes can make a meaningful difference in cancer cell activity. It is known that the higher the quality of the oil, the higher the concentrations of polyphenols. You'll know you're tasting such an oil by the characteristic "tingly burn" at the back of the throat, for which those cancer-busting polyphenols are responsible. Does your olive oil give you tingles? It should!

Olive oil is also a critical component of the Mediterranean diet's impact on diabetes. An interesting study conducted in Rome observed blood sugar and triglyceride levels in two groups that ate the same Mediterranean lunch (vegetables, fruit, fish, legumes), but one group added 10 grams of olive oil, while the other group added 10 grams of corn oil. They found that the olive oil group had much lower rises in blood sugar following the meal compared to the corn oil group, and they also had lower levels of LDL, or "bad" cholesterol. So it seems that it's the specific combination of a Mediterranean diet plus olive oil that makes the difference.

Olive oil also aids in the prevention and management of diabetes. In a study comparing olive oil consumption with the risk of developing type 2 diabetes, participants who consumed the highest amount had a 16 percent reduced risk of developing the disease. But just as notably, participants who had already developed type 2 diabetes significantly reduced their hemoglobin A1c and fasting glucose levels (measures of blood sugar) by supplementing with olive oil.

And the health benefits of olive oil extend beyond blood sugar control. People with diabetes are more susceptible to amyloid diseases (conditions like Alzheimer's disease) because of insulin resistance and inflammation. Emerging research in animal studies has shown that a polyphenol in olive oil, OLE (oleuropein), can reduce amyloid production and inflammation associated with neurogenerative disease.

How does olive oil achieve these amazing results? First, it increases insulin levels in the body by protecting insulin-producing cells. And second, its potent antioxidants reduce oxidative stress—or the cellular damage that results from high blood sugar levels. Finally, olive oil is highly anti-inflammatory. Olive oil contains numerous anti-inflammatory polyphenols, but one in particular, oleocanthal, showed anti-inflammatory effects that were similar to ibuprofen.

Time and again, we see that olive oil is one of the most powerful foods to add to our diet. The same properties of olive oil that fight other forms of chronic disease also apply to joint health.

Osteoarthritis, the most common form of arthritis, is caused when the cartilage between joints wears down over time—typically because of aging or overuse. Common treatments include topical or oral over-the-counter analgesics (like ibuprofen) or steroids. But there is now evidence to suggest that in the future, we may be taking a shot of olive oil or rubbing it on our joints instead! In one interesting study of Iranian women with arthritis, a test group rubbed olive oil on affected joints three times a day for four weeks, while the other group used a topical analgesic. Amazingly, the olive oil seemed to offer more pain relief than the analgesic, and the effects were seen in as little as two weeks! And other studies of participants who consumed olive extracts for arthritis showed the same pain-relieving benefits.

Once again, it's olive oil's polyphenols that promote these anti-inflammatory and antioxidant effects. Two polyphenols in particular, oleocanthal and hydroxytyrosol, seem to be important when it comes to arthritis. As mentioned above, treatment with oleocanthal showed effects similar to NSAID (nonsteroidal anti-inflammatory drugs) pain relievers. And it actually works in the same way—by reducing the production of inflammatory enzymes. The researchers of that study also noted that the intensity of the "throaty bite" in olive oil is directly related to the amount of oleocanthal it contains. The evidence is so compelling that the American Arthritis Foundation states that 3.5 tablespoons of EVOO is equivalent to 200 milligrams of ibuprofen—and without the dangerous side effects! But hydroxytyrosol also plays a role in combating arthritis because it reduces oxidative stress in cartilage cells, which can slow down the disease's progression.

While osteoarthritis is the most common joint disease, rheumatoid arthritis (actually an autoimmune disease) can also affect joint health. But olive oil seems to help with rheumatoid arthritis as well and through the same mechanisms—by reducing inflammation and oxidative stress.

Olive oil has been highly prized by the Greeks since antiquity, but scientific researchers seem to be just now uncovering what Greeks must have known intuitively millennia ago. And while we still have more to learn about how far olive oil can go in supporting and preventing chronic health problems, it's easier than ever to imagine a future in which olive oil is both food and medicine.

and the Greeks take pride in producing very high-quality olive oils. In fact, much of Greece's oil is produced from small family-owned farms that have operated for generations. And quality is actually key when considering olive oil's health benefits—not all oils are created equal. Both the olives themselves and the production process play an important role in how nourishing the final product is, as the oil can degrade by exposure to heat, light, and other environmental factors.

I only use extra-virgin oil, which simply means that the oil is unrefined. This preserves the health-promoting polyphenols, or antioxidant compounds, of the oil.

Polyphenol concentration can vary widely among different varieties of olives. The olive oil produced in Greece most commonly comes from the Koroneiki olive, which has one of the highest concentrations of polyphenols. Like wine, olive oil develops unique characteristics depending on the variety and terroir (essentially the microclimate and soil of a particular place), so it's helpful to consider an oil's flavor profile when selecting it for particular dishes or uses in the kitchen. Mostly, it's a matter of personal preference, whether one prefers olive oils that are fruity, full-bodied, or imbued with the pronounced (and pleasant) bitterness that comes from pressing unripe, early-harvest olives. The "tingle" in the back of the throat that we often sense with good olive oils is the by-product of the oils' polyphenols.

In Greece, we also have a whole category of dishes called *ladera*, meaning "in oil." At their most basic, these are (primarily vegetable) dishes cooked in olive oil to create a rich sauce and make them more filling because they are typically served as main courses. After cooking, we usually add another drizzle of oil for good measure. If you would like to develop a more plant-based diet, *ladera* dishes are a great place to start. Their richness and satiety can win over even die-hard meat eaters. Dishes like the Braised Cauliflower with Olives & Cinnamon (page 227) and Dried Fava Stew with Onions, Cumin & Mint (page 140) are examples of these *ladera* dishes, but with a modern spin.

Sea Salt

Hippocrates (460–375 BCE), the father of medicine, wrote about the efficacy of sea salt for good thyroid function. In a country with one of the longest coastlines in the world, it stands to reason that sea salt has always been part of the Greek diet. A fellow Ikarian and world-class athlete, Dean Karnazes, first hooked me on sea salt when he casually mentioned that it is a great source of electrolytes, the essential minerals our bodies need and often lose when we sweat or urinate during a workout or after, say, too much alcohol consumption.

Sea salt and table salt differ in several ways. Table salt comes from salt mines and is heavily processed, its minerals stripped out and replaced with additives. Sea salt is exactly that: the salt left over after seawater has evaporated. On Ikaria, many people, myself included, collect it in the small natural salt basins that have formed along the island's rocky coastline over eons.

I like sea salt for a simple reason, beyond anything that has to do with nutrition. It tastes better than regular table salt, and that is because one can actually taste the minerals that are still part of its makeup. Sea salt is sweeter and more complex on the palate.

According to the Mayo Clinic, depending on where it is harvested, sea salt can contain up to seventy-five minerals and trace elements. The most basic are sodium and chloride, which make up most of what salt is and which our bodies need to function normally and absorb nutrients. Among the next-most prevalent minerals in sea salt are potassium, which helps regulate our heartbeat, muscle, and nerve function, and helps us synthesize protein and metabolize carbs, as well as magnesium and calcium, vital for energy production and bone health, respectively. Sulfur is another important mineral in sea salt for boosting immunity and helping get rid of toxins. It is essential to our metabolism and heart health.

Most of the recipes in this book call for sea salt. I would highly recommend any of the sea salts harvested in the Aegean. Greek sea salt is particularly rich in trace minerals, which give it a complex flavor and discernable sweetness.

Natural Sweeteners

HONEY

Greek honey just might be the most versatile natural sweetener in the world. It's one of the key ingredients in the Mediterranean diet, appearing in many different dishes, both savory and sweet. Honey is one of the most important ingredients in the Ikarian pantry and one of my personal favorites. Consuming it daily is one of the longevity secrets of the islanders. Many people eat a spoonful of honey every morning. Honey has medicinal qualities. It's antibacterial, rich in antioxidants and flavonoids, and helps the body to regulate blood sugar levels. This makes it the perfect way to naturally sweeten just about any recipe.

Honey allows you to have the best of both worlds. Although honey contains simple sugars, it bears little resemblance to white sugar or artificial sweeteners. Its combination of fructose and glucose allows the body to better regulate blood sugar levels—in fact, ancient Olympic athletes used to eat honey and dried figs to bump up their performance! So feel free to add a liberal drizzle to your tea or a breakfast smoothie bowl, or to whisk it into dressings.

PETIMEZI

I love the minerally flavor of deep, dark, dense *petimezi*, which is, like honey, one of the world's oldest natural sweeteners. *Petimezi* is grape molasses, made by cooking down grape must from just-pressed grapes before it starts to ferment into wine. *Petimezi* is rich in antioxidants; vitamins A, C, and B; and minerals such as potassium, iron, calcium, and magnesium. Our bodies metabolize the natural sugars in *petimezi* easily, too. It's one of my secret ingredients in all sorts of recipes, from tomato-based dishes to salad dressings, and it adds depth of flavor and a very subtle underlying sweetness that helps balance and round out the flavors in many dishes.

A WORD ABOUT DAIRY
CHEESES OF THE TRADITIONAL AND NONDAIRY VARIETIES

In a book inspired by the foodways of Blue-Zone Ikaria, I have included some cheese because it's an important local food, with two major distinctions: Almost all the cheese Ikarians make and eat is produced with goat's milk or a combination of goat's and sheep's milk (like feta), and much of it is naturally fermented.

Over the years of teaching mostly Americans who come to my classes, I've had many guests who are lactose intolerant but are able to enjoy the island's traditional goat's milk cheeses and even a glass or two of fresh goat's milk without a problem. That's because goat's milk contains a lot less lactose than cow's milk and also has a different protein structure, which makes it easier to digest.

Goat's milk cheese is an excellent source of protein, and it contains healthy fats and plenty of vitamins and minerals. Goat's milk also contains capric acid, which may be antibacterial and help fight inflammation. It is digested quickly, so eating a little goat's milk cheese provides an immediate source of energy that keeps us sated for a while. But perhaps most important of all, goat's milk cheeses contain probiotics, which we need for good gut health.

Most Greek cheese is produced from a combination of sheep's and goat's milk. The former, although it does contain lactose, still provides an alternative for people who may be sensitive to the proteins and fats in cow's milk.

Almost all the cheese recommended in the recipes for an Ikarian way of eating are made of goat's milk or a combination of goat's and sheep's milk. Feta is the most common, and it's a naturally fermented cheese, so it has the added benefit of all those great probiotics. You can also find pure goat's milk feta imported from Greece stateside.

As for nondairy cheeses, any substitutes I recommend are always produced with cashew milk. Cashew milk is higher in calories than almond milk and doesn't contain as much protein as soy milk, but it is rich in monounsaturated fats and antioxidants. The milk is produced by soaking the nuts overnight in water, one part nuts to four parts water, then draining and pureeing the soaked nuts with two parts water at a very high speed. The cheese is made by adding nutritional yeast, active live bacteria, and other ingredients to the cashew milk and letting it ferment. To my palate, of all the vegan cheeses I have tasted, cashew milk cheese comes closest to the real thing.

Dried Fruits

Figs and raisins are two dried fruits I always have on hand to use in all sorts of savory dishes, especially in salads and rice dishes. The two best-known and readily available Greek fig varieties are the dark, bronze-hued, chewy kalamata figs and a lighter, softer fig from either Kymi or Taxiarchis in Evia. Dried figs are an important part of the Ikaria diet; people pick them and dry them on low-lying rooftops or in shallow pans in the sun at the end of the summer when they're at their peak, then bake them a little to dry out further and kill any bugs or bacteria that might be on them. Most Greek dried figs are flavored with one or another dried herbs such as bay leaves or, in the case of Ikaria, dried hand-picked oregano.

Yogurt

Yogurt is an ancient, fermented food that has been part of the culinary tapestry of the Eastern Mediterranean for thousands of years. The traditional yogurt on Ikaria is produced with goat's milk and has a delicious sour flavor and creamy texture and is a probiotic bomb!

While goat's milk yogurt may or may not be to your liking—it is exceedingly sour—the Greek yogurt commonly found in American supermarkets is produced with live cultures that make it rich in probiotics. One thing to look for when choosing a Greek yogurt is the Live and Active Cultures seal from the National Yogurt Association, an assurance that you'll be getting plenty of probiotics in a cup of plain yogurt.

Greek yogurt is generally considered to be one of the healthiest dairy products. A half cup contains 8 percent of our daily calcium requirement and is packed with minerals like phosphorus, selenium, and zinc, and is a good source of vitamins B12, B2, and B5.

I admit to a preference for full-fat Greek yogurt, but the low-fat variety has many of the same nutritional benefits.

hospitality
on a plate

MEZE INSPIRED BY MY IKARIAN TABLE

A lot of love goes into preparing the small plates—*mezedes* or *mezedakia*, as they're called in Greek—that most Greek and island cooks enjoy sharing with friends. These are plates packed with hospitality, easy to make either in the moment or as part of a plan and to have on hand whenever company arrives. On Ikaria, and in the spirit of the island, visiting someone rarely involves a formal invitation. Indeed, the beauty of living anywhere with this mindset intact is that the door is always open and the spirit of generosity ever present, and it always involves the sharing of food.

All it really takes is a few olives, some bread, a tomato or cucumber, and some wine or *tsipouro* (Greek grape distillates that are like grappa) to make a friend feel cared for in one's home. But in this chapter, I challenged myself to create a selection of recipes for *mezedes* in the Ikarian spirit that are all plant-based, with very few relying on cheese or dairy to be satisfying. Some are twists on traditional recipes, like fava, the classic puree of yellow split peas, here enriched in color, texture, and flavor with heirloom carrots; others are modern dishes with ancient ingredients.

Two personal favorites are the Roasted Carrots with Honey, Olives, and Garlic and the Pan Shaken Brussels Sprouts and Mushrooms. Brussels sprouts are a newcomer to Ikarian gardens, despite the importance of so many other brassicas in the local diet.

Creating a small-plate experience, though, requires more than just a few fun and delicious recipes. Pantry staples are important, if for nothing else than to provide an instant snack for impromptu or otherwise visits from friends. We eat a lot of probiotic foods on the island, many of which we make from scratch. Home-cured olives and fermented vegetables, especially cucumbers, in simple salt brines with herbs and spices; sun-dried (or dehydrated) produce, including tomatoes, zucchini, and eggplant slices; summer apples and pears, apricots, and more are among the traditional offerings that take time to prepare but are quick to serve (and eat).

My personal "hospitality" pantry includes all of the above in various renditions: for example, green, black, and wrinkled olives, some steeped in brine, others brined then set to float in deliciously viscous Greek olive oil and perked up by herbs and a few spices. For a few years, I became somewhat obsessed with pickling, mostly as a way to keep up with more cucumbers than I could possibly eat. My neighbors didn't want them either because they were overwhelmed by exactly the same abundance. So cucumbers got their salt brine—vinegar kills the probiotics—and they also got a rainbow of seasonings and additions, such as garden dill, peppercorns, red pepper strips, and wild fennel. I still have a dozen Mason jars packed with them in my Athenian fridge. They make a great meze!

Bready things are always on hand, too. While it's hard to surpass the quality of fresh bread from my village bakery in Agios Dimitrios, I always have a kitchen drawer filled with rusks made from barley, rye, wheat, and sometimes chickpea flour. They need to be dipped in a little water to rehydrate, but they are a substantial nibble that staves off hunger and absorbs alcohol, should one be so inclined to serve that to a friend. Wink, wink.

I am placing less emphasis on cheese and dairy than I normally would since this book focuses mostly on plant-based choices. But I always have a little cheese and Greek yogurt on hand and will whip something up or cut up a few wedges as needed. I don't recommend plant-based cheeses as a go-to option for creating a meze spread, because I haven't yet made that personal leap of faith or found plant-based cheeses that truly satisfy my palate. A few of the cashew-milk cheeses come close, though. I'd rather eat less cheese made from real milk than plant-based cheese that tries hard to be interchangeable with the real thing. But, again, that's a personal choice and a nod to Greek traditions, even if those are also changing. The cheese traditions in Greece are very ancient and most often rely on milk from sheep and/or goats, which is easier to digest even for the lactose intolerant.

In the spirit of Ikarian hospitality, and without going to too much trouble, it's easy to have a few jars of good-quality olives, preserved vegetables, and other treats on hand. Those are the bones, so to speak, upon which to dress the table for convivial occasions with friends, whether impromptu or planned. Enjoy!

heirloom carrot fava

Fava, a reduction of cooked yellow split peas, is a Greek classic and one of the most essential plant-based, legume-based spreads on the Greek table. It is an ancient food in the Eastern Mediterranean, and there are many variations. In this version, I add heirloom carrots, which lend both a deeper golden color to the dish and a discernible natural sweetness. Fava is very versatile. You can eat it on its own or pair it with everything from Jammy Braised Chestnuts & Onions (page 217) to the Pan Shaken Brussels Sprouts & Mushrooms on page 39 to simple cooked greens.

MAKES ABOUT 6 TO 7 CUPS

½ cup extra-virgin Greek olive oil, plus more, as needed for pureeing the fava

1 medium yellow or Vidalia onion, chopped

2 heirloom carrots, preferably yellow to orange, peeled and coarsely chopped

1 garlic clove, chopped

2 cups yellow split peas

Water or vegetable stock as needed, about 8 to 10 cups

2 bay leaves

Sea salt to taste

Strained juice of 1 lemon

FOR THE TOPPING

⅓ cup extra-virgin Greek olive oil

2 heirloom carrots, cut into a ¼-inch dice

10 to 12 pearl onions or 8 shallots

2 garlic cloves, crushed with the side of a knife

4 to 6 fresh thyme sprigs

In a large wide pot over medium heat, warm ½ cup of olive oil and cook the onions and carrots until softened, about 7 to 8 minutes. Stir in the garlic and toss to coat in the olive oil.

Add the yellow split peas and stir to coat in the oil as well. Add enough water or stock to cover the contents of the pot by about ¾ of an inch. Add the bay leaves.

Bring to a simmer over medium heat, reduce, and cook uncovered, until the liquid is almost absorbed, about 6 minutes. Making fava is simple, but you need to add liquid incrementally as the split peas cook, until they're soft and disintegrated into a mealy puree. Add more water or stock, again to about ¾ of an inch over the split peas. When that cooks down and is absorbed, continue the process, adding more water or stock in the same way a few more times over the course of about 45 minutes, or until you can mash the split peas easily by pressing them with a wooden spoon against the side of the pot. The amount of liquid you end up adding and the actual cooking time will vary depending on the quality and age of the split peas. It's important to understand what the final texture should look like: There should be no thin liquid left on the surface, which should be erupting in fat, hot bubbles, and when you draw a wooden spoon through the fava, it should make a clear path on the bottom of the pot. Remove it from the heat and place a towel over the fava to let it cool and thicken while allowing the steam to escape.

While the fava simmers, prepare the topping: Heat a third of a cup of olive oil over medium heat in a nonstick, preferably cast-iron or ceramic skillet, and cook the carrot and pearl onions or shallots for 5 minutes, until translucent and glistening in the hot oil. Stir in the garlic and give it a swirl or two in the pan. Add the thyme sprigs. Continue cooking until the carrots are tender and the onions or shallots are lightly caramelized and soft, about 15 minutes.

Remove the bay leaves from the fava. Have at least ½ cup—probably more—of olive oil nearby, as well as the lemon juice. Season the hot fava with sea salt to taste and puree it with an immersion blender in the pot, adding olive oil and lemon juice in alternating doses. It sounds uncanny and out of character for most cooks, but the real secret to great fava is an inordinate amount of olive oil, worked into it with an immersion blender (or in the bowl of a food processor), and balanced with lemon juice and salt, as needed. Even if the fava is loose, it will firm up as it cools.

Serve the fava on a platter topped with the carrot–onion mixture. Drizzle, if desired, with even more olive oil!

smoked eggplant WITH TAHINI & WALNUTS

I love to make a variety of *melitzanosalata* (eggplant puree) recipes to show my guests how versatile this one simple recipe is. Starting with grilled whole eggplant, I remove its pulp and scoop it hot into a few inches of olive oil in a bowl. A little salt is the only seasoning. As I swish the eggplant around in the bowl, it absorbs the oil, becoming a chunky, silky basic *melitzanosalata*—the building block for all other versions. Tomatoes, capers, garlic, and herbs inform one version; roasted peppers and feta another; and then there's this recipe: a heady blend of eggplant, dark tahini, walnuts, garlic, vinegar, a splash of grape molasses, which we love on Ikaria, and a spoonful or two of Greek yogurt.

MAKES ABOUT 3 CUPS

1 pound (450 grams) Italian eggplants (about 3 to 4)

½ cup extra-virgin Greek olive oil

Sea salt to taste

3 to 4 garlic cloves to taste, chopped

⅔ cup coarsely chopped walnuts

3 tablespoons tahini, preferably dark, from unhulled sesame

2 tablespoons Greek yogurt

1 to 2 tablespoons balsamic vinegar

1 tablespoon *petimezi* (optional)

Grill or broil the whole eggplants. You can do this on top of the stove over a low flame, on a gas or charcoal grill, or under the broiler. Turn the eggplants as they cook so they soften and char on all sides, around 15 to 25 minutes, depending on the size and density of the eggplants.

Remove the eggplants from the heat with kitchen tongs and transfer to a large bowl. Cover the bowl with a lid and let the eggplants steam for about 8 to 10 minutes, so their skin softens and is easier to peel.

Place the olive oil in a medium mixing bowl. Place the eggplants one at a time on a cutting board or plate and cut them down the middle lengthwise. Score the flesh so it's easy to remove and scoop it out and into the olive oil with a spoon. Repeat with the remaining eggplants. Swish the pulp around, adding more olive oil if you'd like, until the texture is very soft but also fleshy. Season with salt to taste.

Place the garlic and walnuts in the bowl of a food processor and pulse on and off a few times to make a coarse, crumbly meal. Add the tahini, 4 tablespoons of water, and a little salt, and pulse to combine. Add the eggplant pulp to the food processor bowl, drop in the 2 tablespoons of yogurt, and pulse all ingredients together to make a smooth, thick paste. Adjust the texture with more water or tahini, as desired. Add the balsamic vinegar and *petimezi*, pulse the mixture on and off a few times, and adjust seasoning with a little salt, as needed. Serve this with raw vegetable sticks or warm pita strips or wedges.

herby greek polenta

Corn has been an important part of the original Ikaria diet, insofar as one can claim that, since corn is, after all, a New World crop. But what I mean is that after corn was established in the Mediterranean almost half a millennium ago, it became something people could easily grow themselves. On Ikaria, a few generations ago, cooks grew and dried their corn and ground the kernels into amber granules. These were a substitute for rice. Cornmeal was a staple, too, called by various names: *aravositaro* or *bobota*, and was used in polenta-like dishes, all creamy and comforting. They'd be made with milk from the family goat and maybe sprinkled with some *kathoura*, the local goat's milk cheese.

I have re-created a vegan version below, but you can easily substitute real milk (preferably goat's milk!) for the almond milk. You can make this a day or two ahead of time and sear it just before serving.

MAKES 4 TO 6 SERVINGS

FOR THE POLENTA

2 cups water

2 cups almond milk, cow's milk, or goat's milk

1 rosemary sprig

1 thyme sprig

2 garlic cloves, smashed

Salt to taste

1 cup instant polenta

Freshly ground pepper

2 to 3 tablespoons extra-virgin Greek olive oil for drizzling (optional)

VARIATION: FOR GRILLING THE POLENTA

2 tablespoons extra-virgin Greek olive oil

Greek sea salt and freshly ground black pepper to taste

Make the polenta: In a large pot, bring the water, milk, rosemary, thyme sprigs, garlic, and salt to a boil, then turn off the heat. Allow the herbs and garlic to steep for 15 minutes and then remove them with a slotted spoon.

Bring the liquid back to a simmer and add the polenta in a slow, steady stream, whisking all the while. Season with salt. Cook, stirring, for 10 minutes, or until thick. You can serve it at this point, hot and spread onto a plate like a comforting cream and drizzled with a little olive oil before it starts to congeal, or you can grill it and serve it with a topping such as Jammy Kalamata Olives with Mixed Herbs (page 47).

VARIATION

To bake and grill: Oil a 9 × 13-inch (22.5 × 32.5 cm) glass baking dish and spread the polenta evenly into the pan, smoothing out the surface with a rubber spatula. Cool to room temperature, cover with plastic wrap, and chill for at least 2 hours. Cut the chilled polenta into approximately 2 × 4-inch (5 × 10 cm) strips. Light a grill pan over high heat and add 2 tablespoons of olive oil. Sear the polenta strips, turning once, until golden and grill marks have formed. Season to taste with additional salt and pepper. Continue until all the strips are seared. Serve the polenta on individual plates or a platter with Jammy Kalamata Olives or any other garnish of your choice on top.

crunchy, spicy greek buffalo cauliflower

I had fun with the idea of turning an otherwise greasy snack associated with chicken wings, tailgate parties, and that cold city in upstate New York into a plant-lover's delight. In the spirit of Ikaria, cauliflower is usually reserved for boiled winter salads and a few aromatic and unwittingly vegan stews (so much plant-based fare is unintentionally vegan in the Greek kitchen). Oregano, mint, *petimezi* or Greek honey, and a splash of ouzo give this a Greek passport.

MAKES 4 TO 6 SERVINGS

½ cup rice flour

4 tablespoons almond flour

2 tablespoons tomato paste, preferably Santorini

2 teaspoons Dijon mustard

1 tablespoon *petimezi* (grape molasses) or honey

2 garlic cloves, minced

1 small red onion, minced

2 teaspoons smoked paprika

1 teaspoon cayenne pepper

½ teaspoon smoked sea salt

1 teaspoon dried Greek mint

1 teaspoon dried Greek oregano

½ cup ouzo

¼ to ½ cup water

1 medium head of cauliflower, cut into 2-inch florets

Preheat oven to 450°F (230°C). Line 2 baking sheets with parchment paper.

Combine the rice flour, almond flour, tomato paste, mustard, *petimezi* or honey, garlic, onion, paprika, cayenne, smoked sea salt, and dried herbs in the bowl of a food processor. Add the ouzo and water and process at medium speed to a smooth batter. Transfer to a medium mixing bowl, add the cauliflower florets, and toss until the florets are well coated with the mixture.

Arrange the cauliflower in a single layer on the prepared baking sheets, making sure the florets do not touch one another. Bake for 20 to 25 minutes, until crisp. Remove from the heat and let stand for 3 minutes. Serve.

NOTE: The spicy florets are really good with a simple dipping sauce made of 1 cup of Greek yogurt, finely grated zest of 1 lemon, 1 tablespoon of olive oil, and a pinch of sea salt.

rainbow chard tzatziki
WITH CRUNCHY STEMS

MAKES 3 CUPS OR ABOUT 6 TO 8 MEZE SERVINGS

1 bunch rainbow chard

3 to 4 tablespoons
extra-virgin Greek olive oil

3 garlic cloves, minced

Sea salt to taste

2 cups plain Greek yogurt

4 tablespoons chopped
fresh mint

Freshly ground black pepper
to taste

2 tablespoons sherry,
raspberry, or good red wine
vinegar

Wash the chard well. Trim the tough or scraggly tips of the stems and discard, and cut the stems off the leaves, reserving them.

Bring 2 inches of water to a boil in a large pot outfitted with a steamer basket and steam the chard leaves until wilted, a few minutes. Remove, transfer to a colander to drain, and leave to cool. If there is an excess amount of water left in the chard, squeeze it out by hand or by wringing it in a cheesecloth.

Mince the chard stems. Heat 1 tablespoon olive oil in a nonstick or cast-iron skillet over medium heat and sauté the minced chard stems with 1 minced garlic clove, stirring to keep the stems and garlic from burning. Season with a little salt. Cook for about 2 minutes, until al dente.

Finely chop the cooled steamed chard leaves. Empty the yogurt into a mixing bowl and mix in the remaining 2 to 3 tablespoons olive oil, chopped steamed chard, remaining 2 cloves garlic (add more if you like it pungent), mint, more salt to taste, pepper, and vinegar. Serve the chard tzatziki on an oval platter or in a bowl and garnish with the sautéed garlicky minced stems.

pan shaken brussels sprouts & mushrooms

There's a great dish in Cyprus called *Patates Antinaktes,* or Shaken Potatoes, which is made by cooking small potatoes in olive oil and herbs and shaking them around in a covered frying pan until they're crispy and tender. There's also a great signature recipe at José Andrés's flagship restaurant, Zaytinya, in Washington, DC, that uses a similar technique with Brussels sprouts. I encountered this dish in the fall of 2022 when I was in the restaurant doing an event. So, coming full circle and back to my own kitchen, I've taken the liberty of re-creating shaken Brussels sprouts and including a favorite Ikarian ingredient, mushrooms, of which there are many right around the same time of year that Brussels sprouts and all brassica members start to pop up in the garden. Try experimenting with different mushrooms, such as porcini or morels, and adding a hint of Greek feta to this for extra zing.

MAKES 6 SERVINGS

3 cups trimmed Brussels sprouts

½ pound (225 g) white button or cremini mushrooms

3 tablespoons extra-virgin Greek olive oil

3 garlic cloves, minced

1 1-inch (2.5 cm) strip orange zest

1 star anise

6 thyme sprigs

½ cup dry white wine

Sea salt and freshly ground black pepper

Smoked sea salt to finish

Trim the tough root ends off of the Brussels sprouts. Halve them if they're large.

Wipe the mushrooms dry with a kitchen towel and halve them lengthwise, with the stem intact. If they're large, quarter them.

Heat the olive oil in a large skillet over medium heat and add the Brussels sprouts. Place a lid over the frying pan and cook the Brussels sprouts, shaking the pan back and forth over the heat every so often, for about 8 minutes, or until they start to brown, crisp a little, and soften.

Stir in the garlic and give it a swirl for a minute or so to soften as well.

Add the mushrooms to the pan. Stir in the orange zest, star anise, and thyme. Add the wine. Season with salt and pepper. Cover and let cook for 8 to 10 minutes, or until the Brussels sprouts are tender and the mushrooms are cooked but not mushy. Finish with a pinch of smoked sea salt and serve.

VARIATION

Make this creamy! Combine 1 tablespoon of olive oil, 3 tablespoons of Greek feta, and 1 to 2 tablespoons unsweetened almond milk or light cream in a small skillet and heat over low heat, whisking, until the feta melts and the mixture is smooth and creamy. Pour this into the Brussels sprouts–mushroom mixture, heat all together over low heat for about a minute, stirring gently, and serve.

baked chickpea–pumpkin patties

WITH MINT

Waste not, want not! That's the motto that many of us who try to live a more sustainable life turn to for guidance. This recipe is a Greek island delight created in the Greek American kitchen of Anna Voiklis, who was born on the island of Nyssiros. Not wanting to throw away a Halloween jack-o'-lantern her grandkids had made, she took a cue from the many vegetable patties native to her island, especially those made with chickpeas, a favorite ingredient in the Dodecanese. This Greek American hybrid has all the makings of a great Mediterranean diet recipe. You can prepare it with or without cheese, as you like.

MAKES ABOUT 20 TO 24 PATTIES

3 cups grated raw pumpkin

Salt to taste

2 cups cooked chickpeas (good-quality canned are fine)

1 large red onion, finely chopped

2 garlic cloves, minced

1 bunch fresh mint or dill, leaves only, finely chopped

Pepper to taste

1 large egg, slightly beaten (see Note)

½ to 1 cup plain dried bread crumbs, as needed

All-purpose flour, as needed

½ cup or more extra-virgin Greek olive oil for drizzling or brushing

⅔ cup crumbled Greek feta (optional)

½ cup grated Kefalotyri, Kefalograviera, Parmigiano, or Romano cheese (optional)

Preheat the oven to 350°F (175°C) and line two baking sheets with parchment paper. Grate the raw pumpkin on the coarse side of a hand grater or in a food processor using the grating attachment. Remove and place in a colander with a pinch of salt, kneading it and pushing it down into the colander to release as much liquid as possible. Then place the wilted, kneaded pumpkin inside a cotton or muslin tea towel or cheesecloth and wring it repeatedly to squeeze out all the liquid. Place the grated pumpkin in a mixing bowl.

Drain and rinse the cooked chickpeas. Place them on a large plate and pat them dry with a kitchen towel. Transfer them to the bowl of a food processor and pulse on and off until the chickpeas are mealy. Don't process them so much that they become a paste. Transfer them to the mixing bowl with the pumpkin.

Add the chopped onions, garlic, mint or dill, a pinch more salt, and pepper. If using cheese, add it now. Knead the mixture slightly to combine all the ingredients. Add the beaten egg or egg substitute mentioned below and work it into the mixture. Depending on how loose or dense the mixture is, add bread crumbs and a little flour incrementally. Test the density and texture by forming a 2-inch patty in your hand; if it holds together, the mixture is ready.

Using either a small ice cream scoop or a tablespoon, scoop out equal mounds of the mixture and shape them into equal-size balls before flattening them into little patties,

about 1½ to 2 inches in diameter. Place them on the lined baking sheets about a half inch apart. Repeat until the mixture is all used up.

Brush the surface of the patties with a little olive oil and bake them until golden and crisp, about 12 to 15 minutes, turning them once in the process to brown on both sides.

Remove and serve warm or at room temperature.

NOTE: You can substitute the egg with 1 tablespoon extra-virgin Greek olive oil whisked with 2 teaspoons of baking powder and 2 teaspoons of water.

You can also pan-fry these in olive oil. To do so, season about 2 cups of all-purpose flour with salt and pepper and spread it onto a plate. Heat about a half inch of olive oil in a wide skillet and lightly dredge the patties, a few at a time, in the flour, shaking off the excess. Slide them into the hot oil a few at a time, using a spatula, and let them sizzle and fry for a few minutes, flipping them once to brown and crisp on both sides. Remove and drain on paper towels, then repeat with the remaining patties, replenishing the olive oil as needed.

yellow split pea patties

WITH HERBS & SPICES (*FAVOKEFTEDES*)

As I formulated this recipe, I happened to read in *The New York Times* that Americans throw away about a third of their food every year. Waste is anathema to the mindset of Ikarian cooks. Indeed, almost everything finds some secondary use. Some leftovers are used in recipes like this, while food literally cleared from plates goes to the farm animals kept by almost everyone who lives on the island.

This recipe is one such way to repurpose healthy leftover fava. Yellow split peas are one of the oldest cultivated pulses in the Eastern Mediterranean.

MAKES ABOUT 20 TO 24 PATTIES

2½ cups cooked Heirloom Carrot Fava (page 31)

1 medium red or yellow onion, finely chopped

½ cup finely chopped fennel or dill fronds

½ cup finely chopped fresh mint or parsley

Salt and freshly ground pepper to taste

½ teaspoon cumin powder

½ teaspoon cinnamon powder (optional)

½ to 1 cup all-purpose flour, or as needed

½ cup extra-virgin Greek olive oil

Preheat the oven to 350°F (175°C). Line a baking sheet with parchment paper.

In a mixing bowl, combine the Heirloom Carrot Fava, onion, herbs, salt, pepper, cumin, and cinnamon, if using. Mix to combine well. Add the flour in increments, mixing gently. Test the consistency of the batch by shaping a table-spoonful into a patty about 1½ inches in diameter. If it holds its shape, the batch is ready; if it's loose, add more flour as needed. The mixture should be the consistency of slightly loose cookie dough.

Take about a tablespoon at a time of the mixture—you can also use a melon baller—and shape the mixture into patties about 1½ inches (4 cm) in diameter. Place in neat rows on the lined baking sheet. Brush the tops of the patties with a little olive oil and bake until golden, flipping once, to brown and cook on both sides, about 20 to 25 minutes. Remove, cool slightly, and serve.

VARIATION

You can bind this mixture with a boiled, mashed potato instead of the flour, if you like. For a more substantial meal, you can also make these into sliders by making the patties larger. For the 2½ cups of cooked fava you'll need in this recipe, one large boiled, mashed potato should suffice. Serve the sliders on whole-grain bread or buns spread with a little Greek yogurt or good tomato paste and topped with a little baby arugula.

corn & zucchini patties

Vegetable patties follow the seasons in my Ikarian kitchen, and these are most definitely a summer specialty. When my classes run in the late spring, early summer, and September, I usually have more zucchini than I know what to do with. But as the summer progresses, corn grows, too, and there is nothing like the sweet, almost candy-like flavor of super fresh summer corn. Married together in these patties, the result is delicious. Because zucchini contains so much liquid and will keep exuding water for as long as one continues to squeeze it dry, I have found that cornmeal works better than flour in binding the mixture. It also adds its own underlying natural sweetness and subtly crunchy texture to these bright patties.

MAKES ABOUT 20 TO 24 PATTIES

2 pounds (900 g) zucchini, trimmed and coarsely grated

2 teaspoons salt

1 cup fresh corn kernels, from 2 medium-sized ears of corn

⅔ cup crumbled Greek feta

2 large eggs, lightly beaten (see Note)

5 scallions, whites and tender greens, finely chopped

¼ cup finely chopped fresh oregano

½ cup finely chopped fresh mint

½ cup finely chopped fresh basil

⅔ cup cornmeal, or more as needed

Salt and freshly ground black pepper

Extra-virgin Greek olive oil for drizzling

Place the grated zucchini in a colander, sprinkle with the two teaspoons of salt, and knead it against the holes in the colander to get out the first excessive amount of liquid. You can save the liquid if you want and use it in a summer soup. I give it to my neighbor, who mixes it with old bread and feeds it to the chickens!

Next, transfer the zucchini to the center of a large piece of cheesecloth or a muslin or light cotton kitchen towel and wring it dry with vigor! You want to get as much of the moisture out as possible.

To shuck the corn, trim off the base end of 1 ear and hold it upright on a cutting board. Use a sharp knife and slice down the length of the ear, turning it, to remove the kernels. If they come off in strips, just break them apart with your fingers.

Bring 2 to 3 inches of water to a rolling boil in a small pot outfitted with a steamer basket. Place the corn kernels in the steamer basket and steam them for about 1 minute. Remove, cool, and drain in a colander.

Transfer the wrung-out grated zucchini to a mixing bowl and add the feta, eggs (or egg-substitute mixture, below), scallions, corn kernels, and herbs. Season to taste with salt and pepper. Add the cornmeal, a few tablespoons at a time, until the mixture is dense enough for a patty to hold its shape when formed. You can put the mixture in the refrigerator, covered, for 1 hour, to help firm it up even further.

Preheat the oven to 375°F (190°C). Line a shallow baking pan with parchment paper. Take a tablespoon or so at a time of the mixture and shape into patties about $1\frac{1}{2}$ to $2\frac{1}{2}$ inches in diameter, or as desired. Make sure the patties are all about the same size so they bake evenly. Place them on the lined baking pan, in batches if necessary. Lightly drizzle or brush a little extra-virgin Greek olive oil over the surface of the patties. Bake until golden and crisp, about 15 to 20 minutes, turning once.

Serve on their own, hot, warm, or at room temperature. They pair really nicely with Greek yogurt.

NOTE: If you want to substitute the eggs with a plant-based option, whisk together 2 tablespoons of extra-virgin Greek olive oil with 4 teaspoons of baking powder and 4 teaspoons of water. Add half of it to the zucchini mixture and mix. If the mixture holds its shape when formed into little balls, you're good to go.

The same recipe may also be made with grated fresh butternut squash.

jammy kalamata olives

WITH MIXED HERBS

There's nothing sweet in this jammy olive-tomato concoction, but as the tomatoes cook and shrivel and their juices thicken, and as the onion cooks and releases its own natural sweetness, this simple medley of classic Mediterranean ingredients takes on a personality of its own. To me, it's a great example of what the Ikarian—and Greek—palate of flavors is all about, a much more herbal set of basic flavors than spice-based ones.

MAKES 4 SERVINGS

1 tablespoon extra-virgin Greek olive oil

1 medium red onion, coarsely chopped

4 garlic cloves, finely chopped

2 cups grape or teardrop tomatoes

16 kalamata olives, pitted

2 tablespoons capers, rinsed and chopped

⅓ cup chopped fresh flat-leaf parsley

⅓ cup chopped fresh basil

½ teaspoon chopped fresh or dried sage

½ teaspoon dried thyme

1 pinch dried rosemary

½ teaspoon dried Greek oregano

In a large wide shallow pot or deep skillet, heat the olive oil over medium heat and cook the onion, stirring, until soft and translucent, about 8 minutes. Add the garlic and stir once or twice to soften.

Add the tomatoes, raise the heat a little, and shake the skillet back and forth to roll the tomatoes in the oil and blend with the onions and garlic. Cook over medium heat, shaking or gently stirring, until the tomatoes start to burst. Add the olives and capers and cook together for a few minutes for the flavors to meld. Stir in the parsley, basil, sage, thyme, rosemary, and oregano, and cook all together for a minute or two, for the flavors to meld. Remove from heat and serve with grilled country bread or as a topping for fava or creamy or baked bobota, which is the Greek answer to polenta (page 34).

roasted carrots

WITH HONEY, OLIVES & GARLIC

The dance between sweet and savory plays out in many dishes on the Greek table, rendering timeless a very ancient combination of flavors. Carrots are a big part of the Ikarian diet; indeed, wild carrots grow everywhere on the island, their delicate lacelike flowers the stuff of batter-fried delights in the spring, before they open flat into the flower known as Queen Anne's lace. But carrots themselves figure in many dishes, mostly as a classic vegetable in bean, vegetable, and meat stews, fish soups, and lentil soups. I love roasted carrots, even though they aren't a traditional dish per se. This recipe, with a drizzling of Greek pine honey and a handful of whole, thick-skinned, wrinkled black olives, makes a great meze. As for the sauvignon blanc, I recommend it as the roasting liquid because it's the closest wine to the local Ikarian Begleri, which is hard to find outside the island.

MAKES 4 SERVINGS

1 pound (450 g) medium carrots, peeled

¼ cup dry white wine, such as sauvignon blanc

1 tablespoon Greek pine honey

4 large garlic cloves

2 tablespoons extra-virgin Greek olive oil

Sea salt and freshly ground pepper

3 tablespoons wrinkled black olives, such as Greek *throumbes* or Moroccan olives

5 to 6 fresh thyme sprigs

Preheat the oven to 400°F (200°C).

In a medium baking dish large enough to fit the carrots in one layer, combine them with the wine, honey, garlic, and olive oil. Season with salt and pepper. Cover with foil and roast for 30 minutes, until tender.

Uncover and roast for about 30 minutes longer, until the wine has evaporated and the carrots are lightly browned. Fifteen minutes before removing from the oven, take off the foil and add the olives. Continue roasting until the carrots are caramelized. Remove and serve, topped with the thyme sprigs.

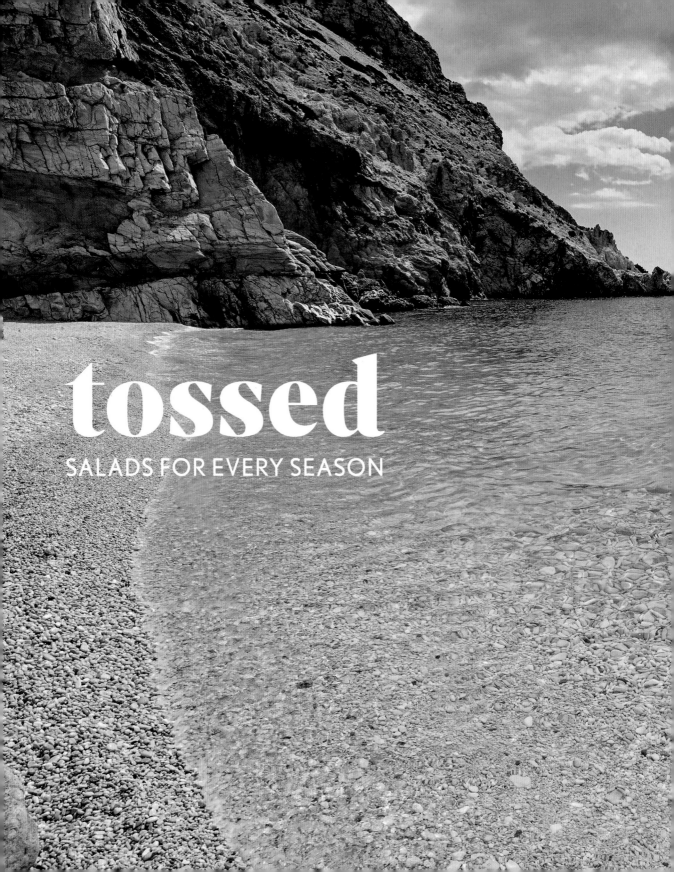

tossed

SALADS FOR EVERY SEASON

I get to Ikaria from Athens sometime in April every spring. We plan and start to plant the garden right around then, give or take a few weeks, depending on the weather. Being a city girl, I am still learning, and my greatest teacher is my neighbor and friend, Armando, who basically plants and tends the entire garden. The garden is the start of most of my salads, and I try to keep that mindset even when I am off the island, in cities, or shopping at supermarkets or farm markets.

Salads are about seasonality, rigorous freshness, simplicity, and variety. I love to mix and match salad ingredients, combining vegetables and fruit or nuts, using twists on simple vinaigrettes, and adding ingredients that will bulk up a salad enough to transform it into a main course. Grains and beans are the main way for doing that, and both are among the foundational ingredients of the Ikarian table.

The place of salad on the table, whether in Greece or Ikaria, is a given. So important a component of lunch and dinner is the salad bowl that meals feel incomplete without it.

Most of the recipes in this chapter are meant to be accompaniments to a larger meal, and most are calibrated seasonally. All produce is at peak flavor when it is in season, and that is one secret to a great salad, whether you're making it in spring, summer, fall, or winter.

Herbs play a huge role in the salad bowl. Indeed, the Greek palate is—again—more an herbal one than a spice-driven one, and nowhere is that more evident than in the generous use of fresh herbs like mint, parsley, oregano, marjoram, basil, dill, and fennel tossed in with leafy greens, cooked vegetables, and more. Herbs are nutrition powerhouses, packed with nutrients and minerals such as calcium, iron, magnesium, and potassium. They provide not only the vibrancy to many salads but are also one of the longevity secrets of the Ikarians, whose use of them in cooking and dried in herbal infusions is a lifelong practice learned young.

To me, salad means variety—variety in color, texture, and flavor components. I love to add a texture to salads and often will sprinkle in a handful of nuts or seeds, both of which are also nutritionally dense, age-old components of the Mediterranean diet. Walnuts, pine nuts, pistachios, and almonds are the most prevalent Greek nuts; pumpkin seeds, sunflower seeds (these rambunctious flowers grow in many an Ikarian garden), and flaxseeds, revered since antiquity for their good nutrition, are frequent additions to salads, both at home and in restaurants.

Some of the salads in this chapter contain cheese, mostly feta because it's the most popular and widely available Greek cheese and also one of the most flavorful thanks to its briny intensity. A little feta goes a long way in perking up a salad. Manouri is another cheese I like; it's similar to ricotta salata and is buttery and mild. For someone looking for a plant-based alternative to cheese, I've included one "brave" dish as far as stretching traditions goes, which calls for tofu, now quite popular in Greece and part of a growing Mediterranean trend.

Salads can be more than a second thought. To make a salad more substantial, there are plenty of traditional ingredients you can work with: beans, legumes, and grains. Chickpeas, black and kidney beans, and white beans of every size are some of the ingredients I use to make a hefty salad. Traditional grains like bulgur and newer-to-Greece grains like quinoa are both easy additions to many salads and will transform them into a healthy main course.

Beyond the litany of seasonal ingredients; nutritious embellishments like fresh herbs; heft-giving ingredients like nuts, seeds, and grains; by far the most important ingredient in all of my salads is extra-virgin—preferably Greek—olive oil. Whisk it with vinegars, citrus juices, ouzo reductions, and more to make a whole rainbow of salad dressings that will add another layer of vibrancy to a bowl of seasonal salad fixings.

A GARDEN OF SALAD DAYS

To get the garden to its peak production, we follow the cycles of nature, of course. In the winter, Armando prunes the few fruit trees we've planted together: apricot, peach, pomegranate, lemon, and navel orange. He takes care of the ten or so olive trees on the land, cutting them back in February, as is the custom. When spring comes around, he turns the soil, a laborious task that involves filling and pushing wheelbarrows mounded with heavy, damp compost, a mix of leaves, and all our decomposed plant waste from a summer's worth of cooking. The garden is spread out over about an acre and is terraced, as are all traditional Ikarian gardens, a necessary landscaping technique that creates arable land on slopes. Armando digs the troughs, which look like row after row of small canals separated by neat mounds. We decide what to plant based on a few things—what the local nursery sells, what he's managed to grow into seedlings from the previous year, what is available at an organic nursery in Athens that specializes in indigenous Greek varieties of all sorts of things, and, finally, what either of us can muster from neighbors and friends on the island who save local seeds from year to year. This last bit usually includes a thick-skinned tomato variety, the fat, pleasantly bitter cukes Ikarians love, called *xilangoura*, and a couple of winter squash varieties.

I head back to Athens sometime after the middle of April and return in mid-to-late May to discover the things Armando has planted just because, well, he can and likes them himself! The lettuces, all floppy and tender as silk, and the peppery spears of arugula, much sharper than what we know in the States because the climate is so much drier and hotter, are always a much-anticipated delight. Those early spring salads are a welcome-home gift to me.

It's not easy to stagger the planting or to know exactly what will come in when because the weather everywhere has become a little unpredictable. But we do count on a supply of tomatoes, everything from those thick-skinned ones mentioned above to a big meaty Vravrona variety (not unlike our Jersey beefsteaks) to plum tomatoes, once-wild cherry tomatoes that we plant from year to year, teardrops, and other, medium-sized round salad tomatoes. I've planted some black tomatoes, too, and I love the acidity and intensity of their juices.

Peppers in every size, shape, color, and heat level are always a part of the garden. A few different eggplant varieties, more cucumbers than I usually know what to do with, zucchini, half a dozen green bean varieties, corn, melons like cantaloupe, honeydew, and watermelon, and then all the edible wild stuff that grows around this cornucopia—namely, *vlita*, or amaranth greens, and purslane, the world's healthiest weed and one we have in abundance in all our Ikarian gardens.

These are the riches that inform every salad bowl. They are coupled with all the herbs that are Greek, as well as additions like nuts and seeds, and some grains traditional and not. I have discovered in my years of cooking that the dressings, which always include olive oil, can be an easy conduit for everything from lemon-feta to ouzo reductions to soy sauce.

In this chapter, you'll find a toss of tradition with a few ingredients from further afield than our terraced land on Ikaria. The real secret, regardless of where you happen to be making a salad, is to keep it local, seasonal, and fresh and to remember that a salad can be a simple—but necessary, at least to my mind—component of every meal or even a meal in itself.

asparagus–strawberry salad

WITH *MASTIHA* VINAIGRETTE

This salad is an adaptation of a dish I love to prepare in the spring on Ikaria, when tiny strawberries first appear in a little corner of my garden and long, thin stalks of wild asparagus rear their flavorful spears in a few distinct places on the island. To go hunting for it is an exercise in mindfulness. What do I mean? Well, city folk like me tend to focus our eyes very differently, and we need to adjust to the rhythms of nature and not to the bustle of a city when looking for asparagus. The spears are camouflaged between a lot of different plants, one here, one there, and you need to slow down and look for them among the greenery. It is precisely the kind of exercise in being present and in walking and stretching and bending gently that is one of the many secrets of longevity here, a kind of walking meditation, Ikarian-style! But alas, we can also easily find great strawberries and cultivated asparagus at good greens markets, so the salad can be replicated anywhere.

MAKES 4 SERVINGS

1 pound (450 g) fresh thin green asparagus

2 cups hulled and sliced strawberries

⅔ cup crumbled Greek feta

2 tablespoons fresh strained lemon juice, or more to taste

½ teaspoon *mastiha* powder

6 tablespoons extra-virgin Greek olive oil

2 tablespoons pine honey, preferably Greek and preferably raw

Sea salt and freshly ground black pepper to taste

Trim the asparagus spears with a vegetable parer and cut away the tough, fibrous bottoms. Cut the spears into 2-inch-long pieces. Bring a large pot of salted water to a rolling boil and blanch the asparagus for 2 minutes. Drain and immediately drop into a large bowl filled with ice water for about a minute. Drain and pat dry.

Toss the asparagus and strawberries together in a serving bowl. Dot with the feta.

In a small bowl, whisk together the lemon juice, *mastiha* powder, olive oil, honey, sea salt, and pepper until emulsified and creamy. Pour dressing over salad, toss, and serve.

What Is *Mastiha*?

Mastiha is a resinous spice from the island of Chios and is one of the most ancient, versatile, and revered superfoods in Greece. You can buy it in powdered form or as crystals, which then need to be ground with a pinch of salt in a mortar with a pestle. Don't use a spice grinder to do this because *mastiha* is a natural gum and will stick to and destroy the blades!

arugula & strawberries

WITH PISTACHIOS, MINT & FETA

I have a pet peeve when it comes to arugula, especially the very thin-stemmed kind available in most American supermarkets: the stems irk me! So I always suggest removing them.

    This simple, vibrant salad is one of many combinations of greens and fruit I love to mix together, and we serve it often in the late May and early June classes in Ikaria.

MAKES 2 SERVINGS

4 cups arugula, trimmed

1 small bunch mint, trimmed

8 large strawberries, hulled and halved or quartered, as desired

3 tablespoons shelled, salted pistachios

4 tablespoons extra-virgin Greek olive oil

1 tablespoon sherry vinegar, or more to taste

1 teaspoon Greek pine honey

Sea salt and freshly ground black pepper to taste

3 tablespoons crumbled Greek feta

Tear or coarsely chop the arugula and place it in a mixing or serving bowl. Add the mint, strawberries, and pistachios, saving 2 teaspoons of the nuts for garnish.

    Whisk together the olive oil, vinegar, and honey, and season to taste with salt and pepper. Toss the salad with all but 1 tablespoon of the dressing. Top it with the crumbled feta and drizzle the remaining dressing on top. Serve.

ARUGULA

Arugula in the US, rocket in Europe, and *roka* in Greece: all are different words for the same wonderfully peppery green, ubiquitous to the Mediterranean diet and longevity cooking. Arugula is a nutrient-dense food high in fiber and phytochemicals; calcium for bone health and nerve and muscle function; potassium for reducing sodium's negative effects; and vitamin C, an antioxidant that helps support the immune system.

Arugula is actually part of the *Brassica* genus, which also includes broccoli, cabbage, mustard, and watercress. And the flavor can range from eye-wateringly spicy to slightly radishy: it all depends on the isothiocyanates, the chemical compounds that the leaves produce. When the plants are growing, isothiocyanates defend them from diseases and hungry insects, but when eaten, the plant gets its many health benefits from isothiocyanates.

The differences in that characteristic peppery taste depend on where arugula is grown.

Temperature plays a big role in the amount of isothiocyanates that the leaves release—most likely, this is a stress response by the plants, and it means that warmer countries (like Greece) generally produce spicier leaves than those in the US.

This gorgeous green is on supermarket shelves everywhere—but it has been an integral part of the Greek diet for centuries. In Ikaria and elsewhere around Greece, we cook it with black-eyed peas and other legumes, but when springtime hits in full force, we typically enjoy it raw in salads.

When arugula starts to spring its tender, peppery leaves from the garden, we pluck them and toss them with a bevy of other delicious Mediterranean diet foods. Arugula pairs well with almost everything that's basic to the healthy Greek diet: nuts, herbs, a range of fruits, sheep's-milk cheeses, and, of course, the most foundational Mediterranean diet ingredient of all, extra-virgin olive oil.

grilled peaches & arugula salad

WITH FETA

The idea of combining fruits and feta or fruits with greens is not new to the Ikarian table. Watermelon, arugula or cucumbers, and feta have long been a most beloved combination. Peaches and arugula make for a great pairing, too. I like to add crunch and a burst of tart flavor with the addition of nuts and a little sharp goat's milk feta.

MAKES 6 SERVINGS

½ cup (100 ml) balsamic vinegar

2 teaspoons Greek honey

Sea salt and freshly ground black pepper to taste

4 firm, ripe peaches

3 to 4 tablespoons extra-virgin Greek olive oil

Sea salt and freshly ground black pepper to taste

2 bunches arugula, stems trimmed

2 tablespoons toasted pine nuts, coarsely chopped toasted hazelnuts, or whole, unsalted almonds

4 ounces (120 g) Greek feta, diced or crumbled

Whisk together the balsamic vinegar and honey in a small saucepan and simmer over low heat until thickened and reduced by half, about 5 to 6 minutes. Season very lightly with salt and pepper. Set aside.

Slice the peaches in quarters and remove the pits. Using a pastry brush, brush the peach wedges with olive oil and season lightly with a little salt and pepper.

Heat the grill to medium or heat a nonstick grill pan over medium-high heat.

Place the oiled peach wedges cut-side down and grill until they turn a golden color and are ribbed with grill marks, about 1 minute per side. Use kitchen tongs to turn them. Remove and set aside. If you are using a barbecue or grill, grill the peaches over indirect medium flame.

Assemble the salad: Place the arugula in a serving bowl, scatter the peaches on top, and dot with the nuts and feta cheese. Toss with 3 to 4 tablespoons of olive oil and drizzle over a tablespoon or two of the balsamic glaze. Serve the rest of the glaze at the table for anyone who'd like more. To store, seal in a jar or container and keep in the fridge for up to a week. Toss the salad just before serving.

garlicky layered two-tomato salad

WITH BANANA PEPPERS & HERBS

A summer at my Ikarian table without tomato salads would be impossible to imagine. While I love the classic Greek salad, a seasonal, juicy, fresh tomato still warm from the sun offers endless options for a salad.

A few different varieties of black tomatoes have been cultivated in Greece for about a decade now, and when I saw them in my neighbor's garden on Ikaria, I knew the time had come to plant some, too! There are many varieties of these dark tomatoes—typically, their skin color is more maroon, but they get very dark, almost black, under the hot Greek summer sun. I like to use the juicy, meaty dark beefsteak in this salad, combining it with bright red teardrop tomatoes, too. The dark varieties tend to have a minerality bordering on salty, and the sweet, small teardrops are like tomato candy when ripe.

Besides being very refreshing and delicious—especially if you're making this salad in season—this bowl of Mediterranean delights is also an antioxidant indulgence! The garlic, red wine vinegar, and fresh herbs are great additions because they're all rich sources of antioxidants, and in the case of the herbs, phytonutrients and vitamins, too. And remember, the darker the vinegar, the more antioxidants it is likely to contain.

MAKES 6 SERVINGS

4 large black beefsteak tomatoes, cored and cut into quarters

1 medium red onion, halved and cut into ¼-inch slices

18 teardrop tomatoes, halved lengthwise

3 banana peppers, seeded and cut into ⅛-inch rings

12 large cracked green olives, pitted if desired

6 tablespoons extra-virgin Greek olive oil

2 tablespoons good red wine vinegar

1 large garlic clove, minced

Greek sea salt

¼ cup chopped flat-leaf parsley

¼ cup chopped cilantro

In a large bowl or on a platter, layer the black tomatoes, followed by the onion, halved teardrop tomatoes, pepper rings, and olives.

In a small bowl, whisk together the olive oil, vinegar, garlic, salt, pepper, and herbs. Pour the dressing over the salad, let stand for 10 minutes at room temperature, and serve.

watermelon pizza

WITH BLACKBERRIES, KIWIS, MANOURI & MINT

The combination of watermelon and feta cheese has been around for a long time. I recall my husband's grandmother enjoying both watermelon and honeydew with feta, savoring the juicy sweetness of the ripe fruit with the contrast of the sharp, briny cheese as one of the great pleasures of a Greek summer. What's essentially changed in this age-old duet is the presentation and embellishments. I have so much fun with this salad in the summer. It's a great dinner party dish because it's so pretty and yet painless to prepare. Look for seedless watermelons and play around with a combination of red- and yellow-fleshed varieties.

MAKES 4 TO 8 SERVINGS

2 1½-inch-thick round slabs of watermelon, from a small watermelon about 8 inches in diameter

2 ripe kiwis

16 firm blackberries or blueberries

16 small fresh mint leaves, julienned

4 tablespoons crumbled feta or manouri cheese

Coarse sea salt to taste

Freshly ground black pepper to taste

2 tablespoons extra-virgin Greek olive oil

2 teaspoons *petimezi* or balsamic cream

Place the watermelon rounds on two flat plates and cut each round into 8 wedges, like a pizza, keeping the circle intact.

Peel and halve the kiwis lengthwise. Cut each half into 2 strips along the rib. Cut each strip into 4 small wedges about ½ inch wide (this will vary depending on the size of the kiwi). Place 2 kiwi wedges flat-side down on each watermelon slice. Place a blackberry or blueberry on each watermelon slice. Sprinkle the mint leaves evenly over the watermelon "pizza."

Dot with the crumbled feta, evenly divided between both watermelon rounds. Sprinkle a pinch of sea salt and a little black pepper over the watermelon rounds. Drizzle each watermelon round with a tablespoon of olive oil, pouring it in a thin ribbon over the surface of each round. Do the same with the *petimezi* or balsamic cream, which is meant to give just a hint of tangy sweetness. Serve.

marinated green bean & tomato salad

WITH TOASTED ALMONDS

Green beans are a blessing and a bane during the summers in Ikaria—a blessing because they grow easily and provide the starting point for many different dishes, from salads to slowly simmered, jammy stews to the vegetable component of more complex one-pot dishes that could include some protein like chicken or fish. But they're a bane because once they start to grow, it's hard to keep up with them. Green beans, flat beans, yellow wax beans, runner beans . . . these are a few of the fresh green beans we love. In this recipe, my favorite is a classic string bean. The trick is to clean them well, especially along the edges so that you don't get a hard-to-swallow thread of bean fiber when digging into the salad. You can make this recipe with good-quality frozen green beans—I do a lot of freezing in the summers and often use my home-frozen green beans in this dish. Make sure the tomatoes are great quality, though. This salad is most flavorful when served at room temperature.

MAKES 6 SERVINGS

1 pound (450 g) green beans, tips and seams trimmed, and halved to get pieces about 2 inches long

2 large garlic cloves, peeled and cut into thin slivers

5 tablespoons extra-virgin Greek olive oil, and more as desired

4 firm, ripe, juicy medium-to-large tomatoes in season

2 tablespoons balsamic or Greek raisin vinegar, to taste

½ teaspoon Dijon mustard

Sea salt to taste

¾ cup julienned or chopped fresh basil or flat-leaf parsley (or a combination of both)

3 tablespoons almond slivers, lightly toasted

Bring a large pot of salted water to a rolling boil and drop in the trimmed and cut beans. Blanch them for 3 to 4 minutes, until bright green, then remove with a slotted spoon and transfer directly to a bowl of ice water for about 5 minutes. Remove the beans and let them drain in a colander.

In a small pot or frying pan over low heat, warm the garlic in 3 tablespoons of olive oil for a few minutes until translucent, keeping an eye on it and stirring to keep it from burning. If it burns, start over with new garlic. Remove from heat and set aside until ready to use.

Core and cut the tomatoes into chunks. I usually quarter them lengthwise and then halve each quarter across the width.

Whisk together the remaining 2 tablespoons olive oil, balsamic vinegar, mustard, and a pinch of sea salt. In a serving or mixing bowl, place the beans and tomatoes. Pour in the softened garlic and olive oil and the dressing, and add the basil or parsley. Toss gently. The best way to toss is by hand. Season with a little more fleur de sel. Let the salad stand for 1 hour to marinate, and toss it one last time before serving. Just before serving, sprinkle the toasted almond slivers over the salad.

lizana's purslane cucumber salad

WITH OREGANO, FETA & OLIVES

I love to introduce purslane, one of the most pervasive—and healthy—weeds to my friends and guests on Ikaria. If you have even the smallest semblance of a garden or driveway with the occasional weed rearing its head, there's a pretty good chance you have purslane growing and don't know it. There's probably an even better chance that you've been killing it off with something chemical, since the notion of eating weeds seems foreign to most people beyond Greek borders. Yes, we Greeks eat weeds, and they form one of the most seminal parts of our diet. In Ikaria, where the flora is impressively rich and collecting weeds is a social activity inherent with gentle exercise like walking and bending and the company of a friend or two, weeds—*horta*—are a much-loved component on the daily table. Purslane is a kind of first among equals by the sheer density of its nutritional profile. It has the highest concentration of omega-3 fatty acids of anything else in the plant kingdom. Snap off its succulent stems from the ground before they go to seed and don't pull it up from the roots, one way to ensure that it will reappear the following year. It grows like crazy once we start watering the garden.

MAKES 4 SERVINGS

2 bunches purslane, trimmed

2 cucumbers, preferably organic

4 tablespoons extra-virgin Greek olive oil

1 to 2 tablespoons fresh strained lemon juice

Sea salt and freshly ground black pepper to taste

6 to 8 sprigs fresh oregano or marjoram

4 ounces Greek feta

Finely grated zest of 1 lemon

Freshly ground black pepper to taste

8 to 10 kalamata olives

Trim any tough stems off the purslane. Cut or tear the purslane into small pieces, about 2 inches long, removing any errant tough little sprigs or stems. Place the purslane in a serving or mixing bowl.

Trim the cucumbers without peeling them, cut in half lengthwise, and remove the seed beds with a paring knife if they are dense and packed with seeds. Cut the halved, seeded cukes into half-moon slices about $\frac{1}{4}$-inch thick. Add them to the purslane.

Whisk together the olive oil, lemon juice, salt, and a little pepper, and toss the salad with the dressing. Let the salad marinate for a few minutes while you prepare the feta.

Pull the leaves off the oregano or marjoram and chop. Place the feta in the bowl of a small food processor together with the chopped oregano, lemon zest, and a bit more pepper and pulse on and off a few times just to combine. You want the feta to be crumbled, not pureed into a paste. Dot the salad with the feta, garnish with the kalamata olives, and serve.

runner bean–potato salad

WITH SCALLIONS, CAPERS & OLIVES

Here is another green bean salad born of my Ikarian garden. Runner beans are one of the great treats of an Ikarian summer. We call them *ambelofasoula* (translated as "vine beans" for reasons unknown to me). Long and thin, these are among the sweetest fresh summer beans and we're lucky—just as they begin to overwhelm us, the potatoes are usually ready to dig out of the ground, making for perfect, and delicious, timing when it comes to preparing them together in cooked dishes and salads like this one. Fresh potatoes are almost good enough to eat raw, and I never peel them, so I recommend you search out small, new organic potatoes with thin skins for the best results.

MAKES 6 SERVINGS

1 pound (450 g) fresh runner beans, trimmed

8 small fresh yellow-skinned new potatoes, scrubbed and rinsed (preferably organic)

3 scallions or spring onions

4 tablespoons capers, rinsed

1 cup kalamata olives or garlicky green olives, pitted

1 large garlic clove, minced

Finely grated zest of 1 lemon

3 tablespoons finely chopped or snipped fresh dill

2 teaspoons Dijon mustard

2 teaspoons Greek honey

2 tablespoons good red wine vinegar

½ cup extra-virgin Greek olive oil

Sea salt and freshly ground black pepper to taste

Cut the trimmed beans in half so that they're all between 8 and 10 inches long.

Bring about 6 cups of salted water large enough to hold the beans to a rolling boil and drop in the beans to blanch for about 3 minutes, until al dente and intensely green. Remove with a slotted spoon and drop immediately into a large bowl of ice water until ready to use. Keep the water simmering, and cook the potatoes in the same pot for about 20 minutes, or until tender enough to pierce easily with a fork. Remove the potatoes with a slotted spoon and set them aside until cool enough to handle. Once potatoes are cooled, halve or quarter them, depending on how large they are.

Drain the beans. Place the beans and potatoes in a mixing or serving bowl. Trim and thinly slice the scallions into rounds, including the green part unless it's tough or woody. I try to use almost the entire scallion in this dish, relishing the visual segue from white to green and how it all looks when mixed. Add the capers and olives.

For the dressing, whisk together garlic, lemon zest, dill, mustard, honey, vinegar, olive oil, salt, and pepper, and pour the dressing over the salad. Toss gently and serve.

garlicky mixed fresh & dried bean salad

Bean salads are a ridiculously easy way to get great nutrition and flavor in simple recipes that take almost no time to cook. I used to be of two minds about using canned beans, but there are so many good-quality (organic) canned beans that don't sacrifice flavor for convenience. Look for low-sodium canned beans for this recipe.

MAKES 4 SERVINGS

1 (15-ounce / 425 g) can kidney beans

1 (15-ounce / 425 g) can white beans or pinto beans

1 pound (450 g) fresh or frozen green beans

3 scallions, trimmed and sliced thinly

1 medium red onion, minced

2 tablespoons chopped parsley

1 large clove garlic

½ cup apple cider vinegar

1 tablespoon Greek honey

¼ cup extra-virgin Greek olive oil

1 tablespoon chopped fresh dill

1 tablespoon Dijon mustard

Sea salt and freshly ground black pepper to taste

Rinse and drain the canned beans in a colander with plenty of cold water.

If using fresh green beans, trim the ends off. Place the green beans (fresh or frozen) in a steamer basket and steam for 5 minutes, or until al dente. Drain and place in an ice water bath. Drain them well and transfer to a mixing bowl.

Add the drained canned beans to the bowl. Mix in the scallions, onions, and parsley.

Make the dressing: Grate the garlic on a rasp over a bowl big enough to accommodate the salad. Add the vinegar, honey, olive oil, the dill, salt, and pepper, and whisk to combine. Add the dressing to the salad and let it stand at room temperature for 15 minutes so that the flavors meld. Serve.

lettuce heart salad

WITH BEETS, APPLES & WALNUTS

When we run the Ikaria classes, Lizana, my friend and kitchen director par excellence, usually makes the salads. She's a wizard with salads, adding what I can only describe as fashion sense—she has a great instinct for pairing colors, for example—to the salad bowls. We're usually at the end of the class and just about ready to sit down for lunch when she discreetly turns her back on the dozen or so guests clamoring around my kitchen counter, and then, a few minutes later, comes out with a stunning bowl of delicious salad. On any given day, it could be anything from simple combinations of tomatoes and herbs to the medley in this recipe, thrown together thoughtfully with stragglers from the fridge and cupboard. It's easy to make this salad in almost any season.

MAKES 4 SERVINGS

4 crisp romaine lettuce hearts

2 cooked beets (see Note)

1 large red apple, such as Red Delicious, Braeburn, McIntosh, or Fuji, preferably organic

⅔ cup coarsely chopped or broken-up walnut pieces

½ cup julienned mint leaves

1 tablespoon sherry or good red wine vinegar

1 tablespoon fresh strained orange juice, or more to taste

6 tablespoons extra-virgin Greek olive oil

Sea salt and coarsely ground black pepper to taste

Trim the lettuce hearts and coarsely chop or halve, depending on the size of the hearts. Rinse and drain well in a colander, then transfer to a mixing or serving bowl.

If necessary, peel the beets and cut into $\frac{3}{4}$-inch cubes or chunks. Add them to the salad bowl. Core the apple, but don't peel it. Quarter the apple lengthwise and cut each wedge into $\frac{1}{4}$-inch slices. Add them to the salad bowl, too. Sprinkle in the walnuts and mint.

Whisk together the vinegar, orange juice, olive oil, salt, and pepper, and pour onto the salad just before serving. Toss and serve.

NOTE: You can buy precooked beets sold in the refrigerator section of the supermarket or simply boil 2 beetroots in lightly salted water until tender, then peel. Don't use canned beets for this. Their flavor just doesn't compare to boiling your own or, second best, buying precooked and chilled beets.

marinated beet & tofu salad

WITH PISTACHIO-FLAXSEED PESTO

In the spirit of Ikaria, I set out to make a vegan beet salad that would approximate one of the most beloved flavor duos in the Greek and Ikarian kitchen: beets paired with tangy feta. As a replacement for the feta, I substitute tofu, which is accessible even on Ikaria these days, and achieve the tangy flavor inherent in Greece's national cheese by using deliciously tart ingredients like mustard, balsamic vinegar, and pomegranate molasses in the dressing. Tofu, the consummate high-protein Asian ingredient, is genuinely easy to adapt to the Ikarian way of eating, despite its non-Greek pedigree. It is mild and absorbs the robust flavors of the Greek table beautifully. As for the pesto, pistachios are one of the great nuts of Greece, a specialty of Aegina and elsewhere, and superfood flaxseed, called *linarosporo*, pops up in salads all over the island. Can I christen this Ikarasian?

MAKES 4 TO 6 SERVINGS

4 medium beets, about 1 pound (450 g) (or precooked beets—not canned!—found in the refrigerator section of the supermarket)

6 tablespoons extra-virgin Greek olive oil

Juice of 1 orange

1 teaspoon Dijon mustard

1 tablespoon balsamic vinegar

2 teaspoons grape or pomegranate molasses

Sea salt to taste

Freshly ground black pepper to taste

1 to 2 garlic cloves, as desired

2 tablespoons flaxseeds

1 teaspoon finely grated orange zest (preferably from an organic orange)

⅔ cup shelled roasted pistachios, preferably Greek from Aegina

8 ounces pressed tofu (see Note)

1 small bunch mint, leaves only, chopped (about ⅔ cup)

Trim the beets and place in a large pot of cold water. Bring to a boil, lightly salt the water, and reduce heat to a simmer. Cook the beets until you can easily pierce them with a fork, about 35 to 40 minutes. Use gloves to remove, cool, and peel.

Slice the beets into $\frac{1}{8}$-inch rounds. You can also use pre-cooked chilled beets for this recipe. I wouldn't use canned beets, though, because they have a mildly acidic, briny, and sometimes metallic taste.

Whisk together 5 tablespoons of the olive oil, orange juice, mustard, balsamic vinegar, grape or pomegranate molasses, salt, and pepper. Place the beet slices in a large bowl and marinate them with half of this mixture for half an hour. Set aside the remaining dressing.

In the meantime, make the pistachio pesto: In the bowl of a food processor, pulverize the garlic. Add the remaining tablespoon of olive oil, a pinch of salt and pepper, the flax-seeds, and the orange zest, and pulse to a paste. Add all but 1 tablespoon of the pistachios and pulse until the entire mix-ture is coarse and mealy, running the processor on and off for a few seconds. Adjust seasoning to taste with additional salt and pepper, and dilute the pesto if necessary with a few tablespoons of water, pulsing after each addition. It should be dense but loose enough to spoon over the salad.

Coarsely chop the remaining tablespoon of pistachios and slice the tofu into rectangular strips about $\frac{1}{8}$-inch thick.

Assemble the salad: Remove the beets from the marinade with a fork and place alternating pieces of beet and tofu on a round platter, layering them concentrically. Drizzle the remaining dressing and the pistachio pesto over the salad and sprinkle with the remaining tablespoon of coarsely chopped pistachios and the chopped mint.

NOTE: You can make your own pressed tofu, too. Buy semi-firm tofu. Layer a plate or pan with some paper towels. Place the tofu on it and cover it with some more paper towels. Place another pan on that and weigh it down with some cans. Leave it for 30 minutes, remove the paper, then, voilà, you've got pressed tofu that can be sliced and diced like cheese!

Flaxseed and Omega-3

Ancient Greeks knew of flaxseed and used it as both food and medicine from as early as 800 BCE. These tiny nutrition-packed seeds are one of the richest sources of omega-3 fatty acids in the plant world. Flaxseed helps control cholesterol levels and prevent inflammation; it's a good-mood food for fighting the blues, and it helps improve metabolism and enhance the immune system. That's a lot of good in a tiny seed!

roasted beet & tangerine salad

WITH ARUGULA & HAZELNUTS

Arugula, which is cultivated in Ikarian gardens but also grows wild on the island, is one of the great super greens of the Mediterranean. Arugula, especially bitter and peppery when it grows in the dry, temperate climate of Greece, is nutrient-dense, packed with fiber and phytonutrients. Our bones, teeth, muscles, nerves, and immune system all benefit from this tender green. This salad is beautiful to look at and has a nice range of textural and flavor complexity, too: crunch from the walnuts and that velvety, slippery texture of cooked beets; natural sweetness and acidity both; and an interesting spice palette. You can swap out any type of orange for the tangerines as well.

MAKES 4 SERVINGS

2 large fresh beets

5 tablespoons extra-virgin Greek olive oil

Sea salt to taste

4 allspice berries

1 star anise (optional)

2 tangerines, plus one for juicing

1 scant teaspoon Dijon mustard

1 tablespoon sherry vinegar or fig balsamic vinegar, or more to taste

½ teaspoon fennel seed, ground in a spice grinder or with a mortar and pestle

6 cups baby arugula, trimmed, washed, and drained well or spun dry in a salad spinner

1 medium red onion, halved and sliced

½ cup hazelnuts, halved or coarsely chopped

Preheat the oven to 400°F (200°C). Trim and scrub the beets. Rub them lightly with olive oil and a little sea salt and place on a piece of parchment large enough to hold them both. Add the allspice berries and star anise. Bring up the sides of the parchment and fold over the edges to seal in the beets. Place the parchment inside a piece of aluminum foil and wrap to seal. Place on a small shallow baking pan and roast the beets for about an hour, or until tender. Remove, cool, peel, and slice into rounds and then into half-moons.

Prepare everything else for the salad. Toast the hazelnuts in a dry skillet over low heat for a few minutes. Remove and set aside. Peel 2 of the tangerines and set the third one aside for juicing.

Cut the tangerines into rounds about ½-inch thick. Light a grill pan or nonstick skillet over high heat and drizzle in about 1 teaspoon of olive oil. Sear the tangerines a little, flipping gently to color a bit on both sides.

Juice the remaining tangerine and strain the liquid into a small jar or bowl. Add the mustard, sherry or fig balsamic vinegar, salt to taste, and ground fennel seeds. Shake or whisk until emulsified.

Place the arugula in a salad serving bowl and toss with the onions and about half the dressing. Add the nuts, tangerine slices, and beet slices to the salad and drizzle the remaining dressing over the top. Serve.

HORTA—GREENS

I couldn't not include a section on greens—*horta* in Greek—in a book that aims to teach non-Ikarians how to emulate the Greeks' foodways. Greens are up there with mushrooms as one of the most important foods consumed in this particular Blue Zone. The island is blessed with an exceedingly rich flora. Wild greens are available for the picking to anyone willing to climb up and down slopes, bend, cut, carry, trim, rinse, and so on, and they number in the dozens, if not more.

To cook them is easy enough: basically, all you need to do is blanch or boil them in salted water for a few minutes and serve them hot or cold with plenty of olive oil, a little sea salt, and either red wine vinegar or lemon juice.

Greens served in a cooked salad like this fall into two general categories: sweet and bitter. Sweet greens include the likes of amaranth (*vlita* in Greek, our basic summer green), wild asparagus, beet greens, borage, chervil, carrot tops, wild fennel, fiddlehead ferns, lemon balm, mallow, nettles, poppy leaves, purslane, spinach, Swiss chard, taro leaves, and a score of more obscure greens particular to this part of the Mediterranean basin. You can mix and match and enjoy a true power plate full of vitamins and minerals.

Bitter greens are a harder sell for our sugar-honed American palates, but they're delicious and extremely good for us. They include things like bitter sorrel (*lapatho*), black nightshade (*styfnos*), which grows wild in my Ikarian garden, and all sorts of greens in the chicory family. We also love peppery mustard greens, cardoons and other greens in the thistle family, and a bunch of local brassicas, like collards and *lahanides*, which are similar to bok choy. Kale is a relative newcomer, but we have embraced it in the Greek kitchen, and I've included several recipes for it in these pages.

Don't mix and match the sweet and bitter greens for the same dish! Sweet greens are also used in savory pie fillings and mixed into bean dishes.

spinach tabbouleh

WITH TOMATOES & PUMPKIN SEEDS

Here's a great salad that's so filling and packed with nutrients that it can easily be a main course. Bulgur, called *pligouri* in Greek, is an ancient food. Pumpkin seeds are lovingly referred to as *pasatempo* in Greek—something with which to pass the time! Joke aside, these tiny seeds—which you should always save when and if cleaning pumpkins—are a concentrated source of vitamins, minerals, antioxidants, and essential amino acids. They're high in calories, but most of their calories come from protein and fats, and only a few spoonfuls go into this salad. They're a rich source of monounsaturated fatty acids and a very good source of the antioxidant vitamin E. If you store them in a cool, dry place, they will last for months.

MAKES 4 SERVINGS

1 cup of coarse bulgur

2 cups of water

½ pound (225 g) baby spinach, trimmed

1 bunch fresh mint, stems trimmed

3 large firm, ripe tomatoes

3 tablespoons pumpkin seeds, lightly toasted

Juice and zest of 1 lemon

⅓ cup of extra-virgin Greek olive oil

Sea salt and freshly ground black pepper to taste

Place the bulgur in a large bowl and add 2 cups of water. Let the bulgur stand for about 1 hour, until the liquid is absorbed and the bulgur expands. Drain off the excess water by emptying the plumped bulgur into a colander.

While the bulgur is soaking, julienne the spinach and mint and set aside. Core and deseed the tomatoes and cut into a ¼-inch dice. Coarsely grind the toasted pumpkin seeds in a small food processor.

When the bulgur is ready, transfer it to a mixing bowl. Add the julienned spinach, mint, diced tomatoes, and pumpkin seeds.

In a separate mixing bowl, whisk together the lemon juice and zest, olive oil, salt, and pepper. Gently fold into the salad. Serve at room temperature.

carrot salad

WITH CARROT GREENS, WALNUTS & MINT

Waste not, want not is a motto by which to live and eat when emulating the Ikarian way of life. Nothing evinces that more than the variety and number of edible greens most of us, myself included, would discard if someone didn't show us a more enlightened way to use them. In the case of this carrot green salad, my ninety-one-year-old friend Yiorgo first explained to me years ago that carrot tops are not only edible; they're also really good for us. Indeed, the greens contain an impressive list of nutrients, including vitamin A, dietary fiber, vitamin C, calcium, and iron. On Ikaria, they are mostly used in savory pies together with countless other wild greens and herbs. I like to add them raw to this carrot salad, a feast for the eyes (literally, too, since carrots and carrot greens are both very good for eye health!) and the senses. The walnuts add a layer of crunch!

MAKES 4 SERVINGS

6 medium carrots, preferably different colors, with their greens intact

⅓ cup extra-virgin Greek olive oil

Fresh strained juice of 1 lemon

Greek sea salt to taste

1 large garlic clove, minced

1 ½-inch knob ginger, peeled and grated

½ teaspoon cinnamon powder

½ teaspoon cumin powder

¼ teaspoon cayenne, or more to taste

4 tablespoons ground walnuts, lightly toasted

¼ cup shredded fresh mint leaves

Remove the greens from the carrots and set the carrots aside. Trim the greens, discard the tough stems, and wash the leafy parts thoroughly, as they can contain some dirt. Finely chop the greens and set aside.

Pare the carrots. Using a mandolin or spiralizer, cut the carrots into thin flat strips or strands.

Whisk together the olive oil, lemon juice, sea salt, garlic, ginger, and spices.

Combine the carrots, chopped carrot greens, walnuts, and mint in a serving bowl. Pour the dressing over the salad, toss gently, and let stand for a few minutes before serving.

warm green beans

WITH CHOPPED ONION, ROASTED RED PEPPERS & HAZELNUTS

Half a century ago, a recipe like this one on the island of longevity would have been quite different: cooked to total softness and speckled with bits of local cured goat meat, called *katsikisio pastourma*, or pork, called *pasto*. Meat consumption was so irregular and scarce that adding little bits of cured meat to vegetable dishes was one way to provide animal protein in very measured doses and to make sure an extended family got at least a little.

For the modern Ikaria way, though, I made the recipe totally vegan. Nuts do the trick, and hazelnuts are really special because they're very delicious, a bit exotic, and highly nutritious. They are an excellent source of vitamin E, which we need to maintain good vision and healthy blood, brains, and skin. Hazelnuts are also rich in manganese and copper and are a good source of magnesium, which, among other things, is one of nature's antidepressants and antianxiety remedies. There are other ingredients besides hazelnuts that you can use to make this recipe vegan, like tofu, for example. As for the beans, go ahead and use frozen green beans if that is easier. They can be cooked directly from the freezer and will need about the same amount of time as fresh beans.

MAKES 4 TO 6 SERVINGS

1 pound (½ kilo) fresh or frozen green beans, trimmed

⅓ cup extra-virgin Greek olive oil

2 to 3 tablespoons red wine vinegar

Greek sea salt and freshly ground black pepper to taste

1 large red or white onion, minced

2 good-quality roasted red peppers in brine, rinsed, drained, and diced

3 tablespoons hazelnuts, halved or coarsely chopped and lightly toasted

⅓ cup chopped fresh flat-leaf parsley

Place the beans in a steamer basket over about 2 inches of water inside a pot. Cover and steam the beans for about 6 to 8 minutes or so, until tender but al dente, or blanch them in salted water (it helps retain their color) for about 3 to 4 minutes.

In a small bowl, whisk together the olive oil, vinegar, salt, and pepper.

Place the warm beans in a serving bowl. Top with the minced onion, peppers, nuts, and parsley. Pour the dressing over the beans, toss, and serve.

escarole & tofu salad

WITH CUMIN, GARLIC & OLIVES

Escarole is a pleasantly bitter leafy green in the chicory family that can be savored both raw and cooked. It's more closely associated with Italian cuisine than with Greek and is a component in the Italian *pasta e fagioli* (pasta and beans) and in Italian wedding soups. I started to use it as an alternative to arugula, which is also slightly bitter and peppery, because it's a little more substantial. I used to make this salad often with hard-boiled eggs, but I have come to embrace tofu and use it in recipes that are part of the Mediterranean and Ikaria diet mindset. This recipe can easily be a main course salad thanks to the tofu; the added protein it provides will keep you full for hours.

MAKES 6 TO 8 SERVINGS

6 ounces extra-firm tofu, cut into ½-inch cubes

1 tablespoon cornstarch

⅓ cup extra-virgin Greek olive oil

2 medium-to-large firm, ripe tomatoes, peeled, seeded, and cut into ¼-inch cubes

½ teaspoon ground cumin

1 small garlic clove, minced

1 pinch cayenne

½ teaspoon sweet paprika

2 tablespoons sherry vinegar

½ pound (225 g) escarole

Greek sea salt and freshly ground black pepper to taste

12 wrinkled black olives, such as Thassos *throumbes* or Moroccan oil-cured olives

Preheat the oven to 350°F (175°C) and spread a piece of parchment onto a small shallow baking pan or sheet. Toss the tofu cubes with the cornstarch and drizzle with about 1 tablespoon of the olive oil. Place the tofu cubes in a single layer on the lined pan and bake for about 15 minutes, or until golden brown. Remove and set aside to cool.

Combine the tomatoes, cumin, garlic, cayenne, paprika, 2 tablespoons of olive oil, and the vinegar in a small bowl and leave the mixture to marinate for 30 minutes.

Coarsely chop or shred the escarole. Wash and drain very well or spin-dry in a salad spinner.

Toss the escarole with the remaining olive oil, salt, and pepper. Season the tomato mixture lightly with salt and pepper. Toss with the escarole. Place mixture in a serving bowl or on a platter, garnish with the tofu and olives, and serve.

kale & cabbage slaw

WITH GREEK YOGURT "MAYO"

Kale is a new ingredient to Greece, and a few friends have started to grow it in their Ikarian "longevity" gardens. It's a member of the *Brassica*—cabbage—genus, and cabbages of every shape, size, and color have long been an important ingredient in the Ikarian way of life, especially in the winter. This salad is a spin-off of a classic winter combination called *lahanokaroto*, or cabbage and carrots, which combine to make what is almost a daily winter salad on the island's tables.

MAKES 4 TO 6 SERVINGS

1 large bunch kale, tough stems trimmed

2 cups shredded white or red cabbage

2 large carrots, peeled and shredded

2 teaspoons flaxseeds or chia seeds

3 tablespoons chopped fresh mint

3 tablespoons plain Greek yogurt

3 tablespoons extra-virgin Greek olive oil

Juice and grated zest of 1 lemon

2 teaspoons Dijon mustard

Sea salt to taste

Cut the kale into thin ribbons. Then wash and drain very well or spin it dry in a salad spinner.

Combine the kale, cabbage, and carrots in a mixing bowl. Add the seeds and mint.

Whisk together the yogurt, olive oil, lemon juice and zest, mustard, and salt in a medium bowl until smooth. Add the dressing to the salad, toss to combine well, and serve.

Replacing Nuts with Seeds

Nuts are such an important and nutritious component of the Mediterranean diet and, of course, of the way people eat and snack in the Blue Zones. Nuts aren't just nutrition powerhouses; they also provide great texture, crunch, and contrast to all sorts of dishes, including, of course, salads. Seeds are great alternatives to nuts for people who suffer from nut allergies. Chia, pumpkin, sesame, sunflower, and hemp seeds are some of the seeds I like to use as nut replacements or just because they're also tasty in their own right. Flaxseeds are a great alternative, too, but to get the full benefit of their nutritional components, you have to grind them first.

chunky fennel & orange salad

WITH *MASTIHA* VINAIGRETTE

Greeks consider *mastiha* their #1 superfood, a panacea that's good for everything from gut health to gum health! But it's also an incredibly versatile spice, pairing beautifully with and adding an exotic, mysterious undertone to everything from citrusy dishes to tomato-based dishes to savory and sweet white sauces to white, milk, and dark chocolate desserts. But what is it? It's the crystallized resin of the mastic tree and a natural chewing gum. It is said that *mastiha* can only be produced on the island of Chios, the only place in Greece where the local climate enables the tree to release its aromatic sap. Greeks have been using *mastiha* for its therapeutic value and as a spice for centuries.

MAKES 4 SERVINGS

2 medium-size fennel bulbs, base trimmed

2 blood oranges or navel oranges, peeled and cut into circles about ¼-inch thick

3 tablespoons fresh strained lemon juice

1 tablespoon Greek honey

Greek sea salt and freshly ground black pepper

1 scant teaspoon ground *mastiha* to taste

⅓ cup extra-virgin Greek olive oil

3 tablespoons coarsely chopped, toasted hazelnuts or pine nuts

Reserve the feathery fennel fronds for garnish. Cut off the root end of the fennel bulb. Using a mandolin or sharp knife, cut the fennel bulb into very thin slices. Crisp in ice water for 5 minutes, drain, and pat dry. Place in a serving bowl or on a platter or large plate. Intersperse the orange slices between the shaved fennel.

Combine the lemon juice, honey, salt, pepper, and *mastiha* powder in a medium bowl and whisk, gradually adding the olive oil, until emulsified and smooth.

Sprinkle the hazelnuts or pine nuts over the fennel and dress with the *mastiha*-honey vinaigrette. Garnish with some tender, feathery fennel leaves, if desired.

farro salad

WITH SUN-DRIED TOMATOES, FETA & HERBS

Adding grains to all sorts of vegetables (fresh and cooked) is a great way to make a substantial meal out of plant-based ingredients. Salads can be main courses, too, of course.

I especially love using farro, a high-protein, high-fiber ancient whole-grain wheat that figures prominently in the Mediterranean diet. In Greece, it is referred to as *dikoko stari*, or double-kernel wheat. It looks similar to barley, though with a slightly more oblong and larger grain. Like barley, farro is deliciously chewy when cooked, and that texture gives it a comforting, satiating quality. Farro and barley can be used interchangeably in this recipe.

MAKES 4 TO 6 SERVINGS

1 cup farro

Sea salt to taste

1 bay leaf

3 cups water

½ cup extra-virgin Greek olive oil

3 tablespoons fresh lemon juice

6 sun-dried tomatoes in olive oil, drained and chopped

½ cup basil leaves, cut into thin ribbons (chiffonade)

½ cup finely chopped fresh oregano, savory, or marjoram leaves

½ cup crumbled feta, for garnish

Freshly ground black pepper

Depending on whether you are cooking whole or pearled farro, follow the box directions for preparing it. If using unpearled farro, soaking it overnight helps to soften it.

In a medium saucepan, bring farro, salt, bay leaf, and water to a simmer over medium heat. Simmer until the farro is tender, anywhere between 15 and 30 to 35 minutes, depending on what kind of farro you're using. Drain and discard bay leaf. Let the farro cool.

In a salad bowl, whisk together olive oil, lemon juice, and a pinch of salt. Whisk to emulsify. Pour over farro and sun-dried tomatoes and mix well to combine. Just before serving, add in herbs, feta, and season to taste with salt and pepper.

lemony marinated raw mushroom salad

Mushrooms have always played a significant role in the Ikarian diet. The island is a mycological paradise, and locals anticipate the first rains and ensuing mild fall temperatures with excitement. Baskets and bags in hand, out they go, foraging for hours, an endeavor that provides gentle exercise, camaraderie, and then, later in the evening, that sense of community and connection as a mushroom feast with friends ensues.

Mushrooms are one of the healthiest foods in the world and are a great way to replace or reduce red meat consumption (they contain many of the same nutritional elements and that meaty texture that's so satisfying). In addition, recent research seems to indicate that mushroom consumption and longevity are connected. The Ikarians knew something about mushrooms, at least empirically, when they set out each fall on one of their favorite pastimes.

Even common button mushrooms, white or brown, are a treasure trove of goodness. They're a good source of vitamin D, an essential fat-soluble vitamin necessary for bone growth and calcium metabolism. Button mushrooms are rich in the B vitamins, and they contain good levels of minerals such as selenium, copper, phosphorus, zinc, and potassium. Eating mushrooms regularly contributes to heart and liver health and good skin!

MAKES 6 SERVINGS

1 pound (225 g) white button mushrooms

½ cup extra-virgin Greek olive oil

2 tablespoons fresh strained lemon juice

2 tablespoons sherry vinegar

1 teaspoon Dijon mustard

1 small garlic clove, minced

1 teaspoon dried basil

1 teaspoon dried marjoram

1 teaspoon dried thyme

Greek sea salt and freshly ground black pepper to taste

2 tablespoons fresh parsley for garnish

Wipe the mushrooms clean with a damp kitchen towel. Cut into thin slices using a sharp knife. You should get about 8 to 10 slices per mushroom.

Whisk together the olive oil, lemon juice, vinegar, mustard, garlic, herbs, salt, and pepper. Pour over the mushrooms. Place in an airtight container in the fridge for at least 4 hours, turning the mushrooms once or twice to distribute the marinade evenly. You can keep the mushrooms in the fridge for up to a week. Remove and serve, garnished with chopped parsley.

toasted quinoa salad

WITH POMEGRANATE, ORANGE & SPINACH

Quinoa, the traditional, ancient, gluten-free Andean grain, has been embraced by cooks all over Greece and fits in well with a Mediterranean diet mindset because it is so healthy. Quinoa is technically a seed. It's a complete protein containing all nine essential amino acids, something rarely found in plant-based food. And if that wasn't enough, quinoa is high in fiber and rich in vitamins and minerals. This salad can easily be a main course!

MAKES 2 TO 4 SERVINGS

1 cup uncooked white or red quinoa

1 tablespoon, plus ⅓ cup extra-virgin Greek olive oil

2 cups water or a combination of water and vegetable stock

Salt to taste

3 cups fresh baby spinach, trimmed

1 pomegranate, or 1 cup pomegranate seeds

1 blood or navel orange

1 small firm but ripe avocado

3 tablespoons balsamic vinegar

½ cup unsalted pistachios, toasted (optional)

Rinse the quinoa in a fine-mesh sieve under running water and drain well. Heat 1 tablespoon olive oil in a medium saucepan and add the drained quinoa. Stir over medium heat for 6 to 8 minutes, until the quinoa begins to toast lightly. Add the water and/or vegetable stock and a pinch of salt. Bring to a boil, reduce heat to low, place the lid on the pot, and cook the quinoa for 15 minutes. When the quinoa is ready and has absorbed all the liquid, fluff it with a fork.

While the quinoa is cooking, trim and cut the spinach into thin strips. Wash it in a colander or salad spinner and drain very well or spin dry. Set aside until ready to use.

If you're using a whole pomegranate, cut it in half across the width (not from stem to base) and place the first half open-side down in the palm of your hand. Using the back of a heavy tablespoon, tap out the seeds into a bowl. Repeat with the other half.

Zest the orange and set the zest aside. Cut the orange into sections. Halve the avocado, remove the pit, score the flesh, and set aside until you're ready to mix the salad.

Place the cooked quinoa in a salad bowl. Toss with the spinach. Add the orange pieces, pomegranate seeds, and grated zest. Gently spoon the scored avocado flesh into the salad.

Whisk together the remaining olive oil and balsamic vinegar, seasoning lightly with salt. Pour it over the salad, toss gently, sprinkle with the pistachios, if using, and serve.

simmered

A FEW FAVORITE SOUPS

The soup pot is one of my favorite pieces of kitchen equipment, a deep well of potential and creativity that also aims to soothe, satisfy, and nourish. The gamut of traditional plant-based soups on the island and beyond includes a bevy of beans and pulses. Lentils and white beans are particularly esteemed. Good-quality canned beans are okay to use, and I do use them in an almost instant *fasolada*, the classic Greek bean soup that's also a popular winter dish on Ikaria.

Bulgur has long been a way to add heartiness to simple soups, and all seasons of the vegetable garden provide baskets full of great ingredients for soups made in the spirit of Ikaria.

This chapter includes soups that go a bit further afield in terms of ingredients. Mung beans and red lentils are now so readily available in Greece that they've worked their way into the pantry of modern traditional cooks. So has kale, which just a few years ago was hardly the farmers' market staple it is today.

The spice palette has changed a little, too. Lemony soups are still much loved, as in the vegan version of an old Greek classic, *yiouvarlakia* (page 109). Lemon and dill, traditional partners in so many Greek dishes, add their vibrancy to a simmering pot of cabbages of every ilk.

I included a few chilled soups in this chapter, too, because they're very old and very contemporary—timeless—at once.

mung bean soup WITH ZUCCHINI & KALE

Mung beans are called *rovitsa* in Greek, and they have been cultivated in the Peloponnese for about a hundred years. They are a favorite among restaurant chefs in Ikaria and beyond who have a keen interest in offering a few tasty options for their health-conscious customers. They are mostly made into soups and salads, sometimes in combination with mixed lentils or grains such as buckwheat, which has also become popular over the last few years.

MAKES 6 SERVINGS

½ cup extra-virgin Greek olive oil, plus more for drizzling

1 large red onion, chopped

2 celery stalks, chopped

2 carrots, peeled and chopped

4 garlic cloves, chopped

1 knob ginger, about 1 inch long, peeled and grated or minced

1 tablespoon turmeric powder

1½ cups dried mung beans, rinsed and drained

1 cup canned, chopped plum tomatoes with juices

6 cups vegetable stock or water

1 strip lemon zest

2 bay leaves

1 teaspoon Greek *boukovo* (hot red pepper flakes), Aleppo pepper, or crushed red pepper flakes, or as much as desired

1 zucchini, trimmed and cut into 1-inch (2½-cm) cubes

2 cups trimmed, shredded fresh kale

Salt and freshly ground black pepper to taste

½ cup chopped fresh oregano or 2 teaspoons dried Greek oregano

In a large pot over medium heat, warm the olive oil and cook the onion, celery, and carrot until translucent, stirring occasionally, for about 8 to 10 minutes. Add the garlic and ginger and stir. Add the turmeric and stir for a minute or so to release its aromas.

Add the mung beans and stir to coat and mix with everything. Stir in the chopped tomatoes, then add the water or stock, lemon zest, bay leaves, and pepper flakes or Aleppo pepper. Bring the soup to a low boil and simmer with the lid ajar for about 30 minutes, until the beans are soft. Add the zucchini and kale, season the soup with salt and pepper to taste, and continue simmering for another 15 minutes. About 10 minutes before removing the soup from the heat, stir in the chopped fresh or dried oregano.

Remove the bay leaves before serving and ladle into bowls, then drizzle a generous stream of olive oil over the top. Serve hot.

red lentil soup

WITH GINGER, TURMERIC & VEGETABLES

Usually when we talk about lentils in the Greek kitchen, what comes to mind are tiny or slightly larger, flat, round, green or brownish pulses. Indeed, lentils—up there with chickpeas, lupines, fava, and vetch—are among the oldest cultivated legumes in the Eastern Mediterranean. Wild lentils flutter among the rich flora of Ikaria and once upon a time were the stuff of a forager's sack. But now the legume world pulses with all sorts of newcomers, at least to island cooks. Red lentils, which made their way into the Greek mindset as the Indian and Pakistani communities of Athens and beyond left their mark on the supermarket shelf and menus, can also be found in the local market in my village. Two other ancient, much-esteemed ingredients add their healthy profile to this soup: *kourkouma*, or turmeric, and ginger, known as *piperoriza*, the peppery root, since at least the time of Theophrastos, the Golden Age chronicler of plants. Turmeric has been lauded for its anti-inflammatory qualities since ancient times and is a spice that many younger, health-minded Ikarians have embraced. Ginger is a power pack that includes vitamin C, magnesium, and potassium. It is efficacious for all sorts of inflammatory ailments, from arthritis to menstrual cramps. And, for any of us who remember drinking ginger ale for tummy aches, ginger does, indeed, settle the stomach and aid indigestion. We mix both into herbal teas as well.

MAKES 6 SERVINGS

½ cup extra-virgin
Greek olive oil, plus more
for drizzling over the cooked
soup

1 large red onion, chopped

3 celery stalks, chopped

4 garlic cloves, chopped

1 2-inch knob ginger, peeled
and finely chopped or grated

1 tablespoon ground turmeric

½ teaspoon smoked paprika

1 medium sweet potato,
peeled and diced

1½ cups red lentils, rinsed in a
colander

1 cup
chopped fresh or canned
plum tomatoes

6 to 8 cups vegetable stock
or water

Sea salt and freshly ground
black pepper to taste

¼ cup chopped parsley,
fresh basil, or marjoram

1 to 2 tablespoons
fresh strained lemon juice

Hot sauce of choice, as
desired (optional)

Heat the olive oil over medium heat in a large pot and cook the onion and celery together until translucent and softened, about 8 minutes. Stir now and then as they cook. Add the garlic and ginger and stir all together for about half a minute.

Add the ground turmeric and smoked paprika. Cook the spices in the onion mixture for a minute or so, stirring, to bring out their aromas. Add the sweet potatoes, stir to coat, and mix in with the contents of the pot.

Add the red lentils, and stir to coat. Add the tomatoes next and loosen everything up by stirring a little and mixing. Then add 6 cups of the water or stock. Bring to a simmer over medium heat, season with salt and pepper, reduce heat, and cook with the pot cover ajar for about 35 minutes. Check on the liquid content and add water or stock accordingly. The soup should be hearty but liquid.

Stir in the fresh herb of choice and the lemon juice. Taste and adjust seasoning with more salt and pepper, as desired. You can add a few drops of hot sauce if you like. Serve hot with a generous drizzling of olive oil over each bowl.

almost instant greek bean soup

Fasolada, a classic Greek bean soup, simmers on the winter stovetops of island cooks who take pains to first soak their beans, then boil them to soften further, then, finally, add them to a medley of vegetables, tomatoes, herbs, and water. Many of my American friends find the entire process of soaking beans just too much work and use canned beans instead. I am embracing that concept! You can use good-quality, preferably organic beans for this soup and other recipes in this book, and there are a few great brands out there. You can also use any other beans of choice, but if you want to keep it traditional, go for navy beans.

MAKES 6 TO 8 SERVINGS

½ cup extra-virgin Greek olive oil, plus more for drizzling

3 medium red or yellow onions, chopped

1 chili pepper, seeded and chopped, or more or less, to taste (see Note)

2 celery stalks, trimmed and chopped (with leaves)

½ bunch Chinese celery, trimmed and chopped, leaves included

2 large carrots, peeled, cut in half lengthwise and then into ¼-inch half-moon slices

2 (15-ounce) cans cannellini, navy, or kidney beans, or a mixture, drained and rinsed

8 cups water

2 large bay leaves

6 fresh or dried thyme sprigs

4 fresh or dried oregano sprigs

1 (15-ounce) can plum tomatoes

⅓ cup finely chopped flat-leaf parsley

Greek sea salt and freshly ground black pepper to taste

1 to 3 tablespoons fresh strained lemon juice or sherry vinegar to taste

Heat 3 tablespoons of the olive oil in a large soup pot and sauté the onions and chopped chili pepper over medium-low heat, stirring, until the onions begin to caramelize, for about 12 minutes. Add the celery, Chinese celery, and carrots, and continue to cook for another 10 to 15 minutes, stirring occasionally.

Add the drained beans to the pot, toss to coat, and pour in the water, bay leaf, thyme, and oregano. Mash the tomatoes with a fork either in the can or in a bowl and add to the pot, or squeeze them over and into the pot by hand and then pour in whatever juices remain. Bring to a boil over high heat, reduce the flame to low, and simmer, partially covered, for 15 minutes, until the beans are completely soft.

Ten minutes before removing from heat, add the parsley and season with salt and pepper. When the beans are done, pour in the remaining olive oil and lemon juice or vinegar. Serve hot.

NOTE: If you want a milder soup with some bite, add the chili pepper whole and fish it out before serving.

VARIATION

To make a thicker soup, puree a portion of it (about a cup, eyeballing the quantity) either in the pot using an immersion blender (be careful to push the bay leaves and herb sprigs to the other side of the pot) or separately in a food processor.

garlicky red lentil soup

WITH TOMATO PASTE, SPICES & HERBS

The secret to this easy soup is to use great-quality tomato paste, which lends an underlying richness and intensity of flavor and also helps create a velvety texture. Greek tomato pastes are typically very intense, with concentrated sweetness and umami flavor. If you are near a Greek shop in your area, look for a tomato paste either from the Peloponnese or Santorini. You can also find both online. Because of the country's dry climate—even more pronounced on the volcanic island of Santorini—plants grow under some stress and thrive in their struggle to survive. The result is an intensity unmatched in most other tomato products.

As for the spices in the soup, cumin is a Greek favorite, and the heat of the cayenne is my own touch. But the herbs are for the most part interchangeable, and that's a general rule of thumb for me when cooking many dishes, on or off the island. Sage and bay both grow in my garden, and we use them a lot. I often approach the use of herbs with flexibility, and you can leave some wiggle room to allow for your own personal preferences, basil over marjoram, for example, cilantro instead of parsley. No matter which one or ones you choose, the end result will be satisfying and vibrant.

MAKES 6 SERVINGS

½ cup extra-virgin Greek olive oil, plus more for drizzling

1 large red or yellow onion, chopped

1 large carrot, peeled and diced

1 celery rib, trimmed and diced

3 large garlic cloves, minced

1 heaping tablespoon good-quality tomato paste, preferably from Santorini or the Peloponnese

1 heaping teaspoon ground cumin

1 pinch ground chili powder or cayenne, or more to taste

1½ cups red lentils

1 quart vegetable broth

2 cups water

1 large fresh or dried bay leaf

2 fresh or dried sage leaves

Greek sea salt and freshly ground black pepper to taste

Juice of ½ a lemon, or more to taste

3 tablespoons chopped fresh basil, marjoram, cilantro, or flat-leaf parsley

In a large pot, heat the olive oil over medium heat and cook the onion, carrot, and celery until translucent and soft, about 10 minutes, stirring occasionally. Stir in the garlic and swirl it around for about half a minute.

Add the tomato paste and cook it with the onion mixture, stirring it to mix in with all the vegetables. Allow it to cook a little, which intensifies its flavor. Stir in the cumin and cayenne or chili powder, again, swirling around with everything else in the pan so their aromas bloom with the heat.

Next, add the lentils and stir to coat in the olive oil.

Add the broth, 2 cups of water, bay, and sage. Bring to a simmer, season with salt and pepper, then partially cover the pot, lower the heat, and simmer until lentils are soft, about 30 minutes.

Remove the bay leaf and sage with a slotted spoon. Using an immersion or regular blender or food processor, puree half the soup, then add it back to the pot. Reheat and stir in the lemon juice and fresh herb or herbs of choice.

Serve soup drizzled with additional olive oil.

lemony bean & brassica soup

WITH NAPA CABBAGE & DILL

Cabbage lovers rejoice! This brassica–heavy bean soup is packed with several members of the *Brassica* genus, one of the healthiest and most nutritious vegetable groups in the world. I can't help but think this soup is like an Ikarian garden on steroids, so to speak, chock–full of various species of these cruciferous vegetables and roots, many of which have long provided easy, inexpensive, and health–giving opportunities to make a delicious dinner that doesn't cost that much or take much to produce in one's own backyard. You can play around with this, adding, say Brussels sprouts or even kale to the soup.

MAKES 8 SERVINGS

½ lemon

1 small celery root (celeriac)

¾ cup extra-virgin Greek olive oil

1 large red onion, chopped

1 large leek, trimmed and chopped

1 small bunch Chinese celery, trimmed and chopped (with leaves)

½ small head Napa or Savoy cabbage, trimmed and finely shredded (about 3 cups)

1 large carrot, trimmed, peeled, and chopped

1 parsnip, pared and cut into a ½-inch (1½-cm) dice

1 rutabaga, peeled and cut into a ½-inch (1½-cm) dice

1 kohlrabi, trimmed and cut into a ½-inch (1½-cm) dice

4 garlic cloves

4 cups canned navy or other white beans, preferably organic

10 cups vegetable broth or stock, or water

2 bay leaves

6 thyme sprigs

Fresh strained juice of 1 lemon, or more to taste

Sea salt and freshly ground black pepper

1 small bunch dill, leaves snipped or chopped

Prepare acidulated water by squeezing and dropping half a lemon into 3 cups of water in a medium mixing bowl. Trim, peel, and dice the celeriac (celery root) and place it in the acidulated water. Set aside until ready to use.

Drain the celeriac. In a large soup pot, heat $\frac{1}{4}$ cup of olive oil and cook the onion, leek, celery, celeriac, carrot, parsnip, rutabaga, and kohlrabi until translucent and al dente, and until the onions are soft. Stir the garlic into the vegetable mixture. Add the beans, stock or water, bay leaves, and thyme. Reduce heat to low, bring to a simmer, keep the lid on the pot ajar, and cook until the vegetables are very tender, about 35 to 40 minutes. Fish out the thyme and bay leaves with a spoon and discard.

Using an immersion blender, puree a little bit of the soup in the pot, about $1\frac{1}{2}$ cups or so—use your judgment to "eyeball" it. Doing this will create a creamy texture. Stir in the cabbage and cook the soup for 15 more minutes, or until the cabbage is tender.

Whisk the lemon juice and remaining olive oil together in a small bowl and add the mixture to the soup. Season to taste with salt and pepper, and stir in the dill. Adjust seasoning with salt and pepper, and serve.

big bean, corn & pumpkin soup

I just love this soup. It's not traditional, in that few of my island friends would think of mixing beans, corn, and winter squash in the same pot, but it's definitely in the spirit of the seasons. At the very end of the summer as the light changes and the evening chill starts to prickle your arms with just a hint of what's to come, the gardens on the island segue from bright greens and reds to more muted shades of ochre. The last tomatoes droop, and their vines are all dried and scraggly, but a whole cacophony of squashes dangle on thick, succulent vines from walls or stretch out over the ground in an effusive web. The corn is also in, and whatever the birds haven't gotten to is a treat for us humans and cooks. And it's as sweet as candy, to be sure. Over my three decades in Greece, I've encountered a number of recipes in different parts of the country that speak to the segue between summer and fall. They usually involve a marriage of summer and autumn crops. Dried beans are an all-season pantry item. This soup reminds me of the bounty of my Ikarian garden just as I am preparing to leave the island in early to mid-October, so it's bittersweet for me as well as soul-soothing.

MAKES 6 TO 8 SERVINGS

⅔ cup extra-virgin
Greek olive oil, plus more
for drizzling

3 large red onions, chopped

5 large garlic cloves, minced
(about 3 teaspoons)

1 heaping tablespoon
good-quality tomato paste,
preferably from Santorini
or the Peloponnese

1 pound
(450 g) dried Greek giant
beans or butter beans, soaked
in water overnight or 6 cups
good-quality, preferably
organic, canned beans,
drained and rinsed

1 cup chopped canned plum
tomatoes

2 bay leaves

4 fresh oregano sprigs

2 strips orange zest

2 cups corn kernels,
preferably freshly shucked

3 cups cubed pumpkin
or butternut squash

½ cup chopped fresh basil

1 to 2 tablespoons *petimezi*
or Greek pine honey

1 to 2 tablespoons balsamic
vinegar

In a large soup pot, heat 3 tablespoons of olive oil and cook the onion until soft and translucent, over medium heat, for about 10 minutes, stirring occasionally. Stir in all but 1 teaspoon of the garlic, give it a swirl or two, then stir in the tomato paste. Set the remaining garlic aside.

To the pot, add the drained beans, enough water to cover by 2 inches, the chopped plum tomatoes, bay leaves, oregano sprigs, and orange zest. Bring to a boil, reduce heat to medium-low, and simmer until the beans are very tender, about 1½ to 2 hours.

Remove 2 cups of the soup and puree in a food processor or blender, then return it to the large pot.

In a large skillet, heat 3 more tablespoons of the olive oil over medium heat, stir in the remaining garlic, and a few seconds later, add the corn and pumpkin or butternut squash. Shake the pan back and forth to combine all the flavors. Transfer the mixture to the soup pot.

Remove the orange zest, oregano sprigs, and bay leaves. Bring everything back to a simmer, adjust the seasoning with salt, and stir in the basil, *petimezi* or honey, and balsamic vinegar. Drizzle in the remaining olive oil, stir, and serve.

vegan *yiouvarlakia*

WITH MUSHROOMS & AVOCADO AVGOLEMONO

Yiouvarlakia (plural), traditionally a comforting combination of ground beef or lamb and rice shaped into balls and cooked in an avgolemono broth, make for one of the great winter dishes of Greece, a treat that Greek moms make for their kids partly for nourishment and partly to bask in the praise that is usually lavished upon them with the first serving! This recipe is different. It was born in my Athens kitchen with the help of Greece's premiere vegan chef, Nikos Gaitanos, and we cooked it together for an episode titled "The Accidental Vegan" for season four of the *My Greek Table* television series. Like so much vegan food in Greece, this doesn't call for anything processed, such as "impossible" meat or any other laboratory-born creations. Indeed, it calls for one of the most important raw ingredients in the traditional Ikarian diet: mushrooms.

MAKES 4 SERVINGS

¼ cup raw Arborio rice

1 pound (½ kilo) white button mushrooms, thinly sliced

6 tablespoons extra-virgin Greek olive oil

1 teaspoon finely chopped fresh thyme

Sea salt and freshly ground black pepper to taste

6 tablespoons all-purpose flour

FOR THE SOUP

6 tablespoons extra-virgin Greek olive oil

2 medium Yukon Gold or similar potatoes, peeled and cut into small cubes

2 medium carrots, peeled and cut into small cubes

2 medium zucchini, cut into small cubes

1 large red onion, finely chopped

1 small stalk celery, finely chopped

1 cup dry white wine

½ cup water

FOR THE AVOCADO "AVGOLEMONO"

2 soft, ripe avocados

Juice of 2 lemons

3 cups of the soup

Salt and freshly ground black pepper to taste

1 tablespoon chopped fresh dill or parsley

Preheat the oven to 360°F (180°C). Line a baking sheet with parchment paper.

Bring the Arborio to a simmer over low to medium heat in a small covered pot with a cup or so of lightly salted water, cooking it until soft, about 20 minutes. If there is still liquid in the pot, drain it out and set the cooked rice aside.

While the rice is cooking, prepare the mushrooms. In a medium bowl, combine the sliced mushrooms with the olive oil and thyme. Season lightly with salt and pepper. Spread the mixture in one layer over the surface of the baking sheet and bake in the oven for about 20 minutes, or until soft and wrinkled.

Remove from the oven and let the mushrooms cool for 10 minutes. Transfer in batches or handfuls to a cutting board and finely chop them.

Combine the mushrooms, cooked rice, flour, salt, and pepper. Knead well until the mixture holds together. Shape into small balls about $1\frac{1}{2}$ inches (4 cm) in diameter and bake at 360°F (180°C) for about 15 minutes or until firm and the exterior is crusty and slightly charred.

Let the mushroom–rice balls cool for 10 minutes, then set aside until ready to incorporate into the rest of the recipe.

Make the broth: Heat the olive oil in a large saucepan over medium heat and sauté the vegetables until soft and translucent, about 12 to 15 minutes. Pour in the wine, bring to a simmer over medium heat, and cook for a few minutes until the alcohol has burned off. Add enough water to cover the vegetables by 4 inches (10 cm), season with salt and pepper, and cook over low heat until the vegetables are very soft, about 40 minutes.

When the broth is ready, make the avocado lemon sauce: Place the avocado pulp, lemon juice, and 3 cups of the hot soup in a blender or food processor and process on high speed until creamy. Transfer the avocado–lemon mixture to the soup, and add the mushroom–rice balls and the dill or parsley. Serve immediately.

creamy zucchini soup

WITH LEMON & GREEK YOGURT

Lemon zest is one of my secret go-to ingredients when I want to perk up the flavor of otherwise mild or subtle dishes. Can you think of another vegetable as mild as zucchini? Lemon is, in fact, as crucial a flavor enhancer as salt and works pretty much the same way on your palate. Both make your mouth water, and the acidity of lemons makes everything seem fresher and more alive. Keep this little secret in hand for many dishes, beyond zucchini soup!

MAKES 4 SERVINGS

3 tablespoons extra-virgin Greek olive oil, plus more for drizzling

1 large white onion, chopped

1 leek, trimmed and chopped

2 garlic cloves, minced

2 pounds (900 g) zucchini, trimmed and chopped

3 cups vegetable broth

1 cup water, or more as needed

½ cup Greek yogurt, plus more, as desired, for garnish

1 cup milk or unsweetened almond or oat milk

Finely grated zest of 1 lemon

Salt and freshly ground black pepper

⅓ cup finely chopped fresh mint

Heat the olive oil in a large pot over medium-high heat. Add onion, leek, and garlic, and cook, covered, for about 10 minutes until soft and translucent. Stir the contents of the pot now and then to keep them from burning.

Add zucchini and sauté for another 10 minutes, tossing to coat in the oil. Add broth and water. Bring to a boil, then cover and reduce heat to medium. Cook for 15 to 20 minutes, or until the zucchini is very soft.

Using an immersion blender, puree the soup in the pot. (Alternatively, you can puree it in a food processor and return it to the pot.) Vigorously whisk in the yogurt, milk or almond or oat milk, and lemon zest. Adjust seasoning with additional salt and pepper to taste. Bring back to a simmer, whisking to distribute the yogurt and milk evenly. If the soup is too thick, dilute it with a little more water or broth. Remove from heat and stir in the fresh mint.

Serve in bowls, swirl in a teaspoon of yogurt or two, if desired, and a little more pepper. Serve hot. Alternatively, you can chill the soup and serve it cold.

sheet-pan portobello soup

WITH WALNUT GREMOLATA

I love the elegance and earthiness of mushrooms in so many different recipes. This soup is something I like to make in the fall, just as the weather starts to get cold. The walnut, lemon, and herb topping, a kind of gremolata born out of important Ikarian ingredients, perks up the soup and balances its earthy flavors with crunch and delicate astringency. Lemon in any way and form is a highly esteemed fruit throughout Greek cooking.

MAKES 6 SERVINGS

8 large portobello mushrooms, wiped clean with a damp cloth

½ cup extra-virgin Greek olive oil, plus 2 tablespoons, or more as needed

Greek sea salt and freshly ground black pepper to taste

3 large red or yellow onions, peeled and quartered

1 whole head of garlic

2 teaspoons dried tarragon

2 teaspoons dried marjoram or thyme

1 heaping teaspoon dried mushroom powder (optional)

2 scant teaspoons all-purpose or almond flour

1 cup dry Greek white wine

1¼ quarts vegetable stock

1 tablespoon balsamic vinegar

FOR THE NUT TOPPING

1 cup finely chopped toasted walnuts or unsalted cashews

1 cup finely chopped fresh flat-leaf parsley

¼ cup finely chopped fresh mint

2 tablespoons extra-virgin Greek olive oil

2 teaspoons grated lemon zest, plus 1 tablespoon fresh juice (from 1 lemon)

1 medium garlic clove, chopped (about 1 teaspoon)

Sea salt and freshly ground black pepper to taste

Preheat the broiler. Line a baking sheet with parchment.

Remove the stems from the portobellos, cut them in half lengthwise if they're thick, and set aside. Cut the portobello caps in half or into thick strips about 1½ inches (4 cm) wide. Place the portobellos and their stems in a large bowl and toss with 5 tablespoons of the olive oil and a little sea salt and pepper. Place the caps and stems on the baking sheet all on one side to make room for the onions. Place the onions in the same bowl in which you tossed the mushrooms and combine with the remaining 3 tablespoons of olive oil and a little sea salt and pepper. Place them on the other half of the baking sheet.

Wrap the garlic head in aluminum foil and lodge it in the center of the sheet pan.

Broil the onions and mushrooms for about 15 minutes at about 8 inches from the heat source, or until charred. Turn them as needed while they broil so they cook on all sides. Remove the sheet pan when the mushrooms and onions are ready, but leave the garlic in for about another 15 to 20 minutes, as it will need more time to soften. You can leave it on the oven rack at this point.

Let the onion and mushrooms cool slightly. Transfer in batches to a cutting board and chop, reserving any liquid that trickles off.

Remove the garlic and let it cool enough to handle.

In a large pot over medium heat, add 2 more tablespoons of olive oil. Add the chopped charred onions and cook for 5 minutes. Add the mushrooms and any pan juices, then squeeze out the roasted garlic clove by clove into the pot. Toss to coat. Season with salt, pepper, tarragon, marjoram or thyme, and mushroom powder. Stir together for a few minutes for the flavors to develop.

Sprinkle in the flour and stir until the mixture becomes a little pasty. Pour in the wine. As soon as the alcohol steams off, add the stock. Bring to a boil over high heat, reduce to medium, and simmer for 15 minutes for the flavors to meld.

Make the nut topping: Combine everything in a large bowl, mix well, and set aside.

Remove from heat. With an immersion blender, puree all or part of the soup in the pot. Add the balsamic vinegar, stir well, and adjust the seasoning with salt and pepper. Serve garnished with some of the nut gremolata.

broccoli soup thickened with nuts

In this recipe, I call for an age–old Greek tradition of using nuts as a thickener. Cashews, while not native to Greece, are a much–loved nut. They are super rich in iron and copper, which positively impacts our metabolism. Cashews boost our energy and are good for heart health. They contain a lot of the micronutrients we need to increase our bone density, which is especially important as we age. Surprisingly, consuming cashews may just help increase our sex drive, and staying active sexually is another one of the longevity secrets of my fellow islanders on Ikaria!

MAKES 6 SERVINGS

1 large broccoli head

6 tablespoons extra-virgin olive oil, plus more for drizzling

1 large onion, chopped

1 celery stalk and leaves, chopped

1 fennel bulb, chopped

1 medium carrot, peeled and chopped

1 medium waxy potato, diced

1 star anise

4 garlic cloves, minced

1 1-inch knob ginger, peeled and minced or grated

6 to 8 cups vegetable broth or stock

FOR THE CASHEW CREAM

½ cup raw cashews

1 teaspoon sherry vinegar

1 scant teaspoon Dijon mustard

¼ cup fresh dill

1 tablespoon fresh lemon juice

Sea salt and freshly ground black pepper to taste

Trim the broccoli: Cut away any tough part of its lower stem but retain the stem because you can use it in the soup. Trim and chop the stem and cut the broccoli into small florets. Set aside 6 or 12 small florets, about an inch or so in area.

In a large pot over medium–low heat, warm 4 tablespoons of the olive oil and add the onion, celery, fennel, carrot, remaining broccoli florets and stems, potatoes, and star anise. Toss to coat in the oil. Cover and steam in the olive oil for 5 minutes. Stir in the garlic and ginger and steam in the oil, covered, for another 3 minutes.

Add the vegetable broth or stock and 1 cup of water. Bring to a simmer, and season to taste with salt. Cover the pot and continue to simmer the soup until all the vegetables are fork–tender, about 35 to 40 minutes.

While the soup is simmering, toss the broccoli florets you've set aside with the remaining tablespoon of olive oil and a little salt, place on a small baking pan, and broil for 5 to 7 minutes, turning, until lightly charred. Remove and set aside.

In a small food processor, pulverize the cashews, vinegar, mustard, dill, and lemon juice to a thick paste.

Remove the star anise from the soup pot and discard. Using an immersion blender, puree the soup until everything is more or less broken down but still coarse. Add the cashew paste and continue pureeing until the consistency is thick and creamy. Adjust the seasoning with additional salt, vinegar, or lemon juice. Bring the soup back to a boil and turn off the heat. Serve the soup hot in individual bowls garnished with the charred florets and a drizzling of olive oil.

herby bulgur vegetable soup

Bulgur, one of the most ancient foods in Greece, was an important staple on Ikaria, too. Wheat was typically grown in small quantities for family use, and you can still see the terraces carved like steps into mountain slopes, making room for arable land where garden vegetables and grains could be grown. Bulgur, as well as dried corn, figured in place of rice before the latter became readily available, which didn't really happen until the 1950s. I love the nutty flavor of bulgur as well as its versatility in everything from salads to soups and stuffings. It's packed with vitamins and minerals and is really easy to use. This is an all-weather soup and is just as delicious hot as it is chilled. You can find it coarse- or fine-grained.

MAKES 4 SERVINGS

⅔ cup coarse bulgur wheat

4 tablespoons extra-virgin Greek olive oil, plus more for drizzling

6 scallions, trimmed and finely chopped

2 cups finely chopped celery

3 garlic cloves, minced

1 cup diced carrot

1 cup diced fennel bulb

Salt and freshly ground black pepper

4 large firm, ripe tomatoes, grated, or 2 cups good-quality chopped canned tomatoes

1 quart vegetable stock

3 bay leaves

6 fresh thyme sprigs

2 fresh oregano sprigs

2 strips of lemon zest

2 to 4 tablespoons fresh strained lemon juice

½ cup finely chopped fresh flat-leaf parsley

½ cup finely chopped fresh mint leaves

8 teaspoons crumbled Greek feta or Greek yogurt (optional)

Hot sauce (optional)

Soak the bulgur wheat in 1⅓ cups of water for 1 hour to soften. It is ready when it's absorbed most or all of the liquid and is swollen and softened.

While the bulgur is soaking, prepare the vegetables: Heat the olive oil in a medium-sized wide pot over medium heat and cook the scallions, celery, carrot, and fennel until soft, stirring gently, for about 10 minutes. Stir in the garlic. Season with salt and pepper. Pour in the tomatoes and vegetable stock. Add the bay leaves, thyme and oregano sprigs, and lemon zest. Season with salt and pepper. Bring to a boil, reduce heat to medium-low, cover, and simmer for 20 minutes. Remove the sprigs, bay leaves, and lemon zest with a slotted spoon. At this point, you can leave the soup as is or puree it with an immersion blender, if you prefer a smooth velvety soup (velouté) to a chunky vegetable soup. I like it both ways.

Add the bulgur. As soon as the mixture simmers, reduce heat to low, cover the pot, and continue simmering for another 5 minutes for the flavors to meld. If the soup is too thick, add a little more stock or water. Stir in the lemon juice, parsley, and mint. If you like spice, you can stir in a little hot sauce.

Serve hot, garnished with a little Greek yogurt or feta swirled in, if desired, and drizzled generously with more olive oil.

chilled cucumber–yogurt–avocado soup

If you've ever experienced the cooling effects of *aryani* or kefir on a hot summer day, you will appreciate this recipe, which falls somewhere between a chilled soup and a savory smoothie. Refreshing yogurt drinks have been enjoyed in the Eastern Mediterranean and Balkans for as long as there have been shepherds roaming the mountains, basically forever! But avocados are an import, the very closest point of departure being the island of Crete, where they have been cultivated for a few decades. The combination of smooth-textured ripe avocados and tangy Greek yogurt is a perfect match.

MAKES 4 SERVINGS

2 large spring onions, trimmed and coarsely chopped

1 garlic clove, minced

4 large cucumbers, peeled, seeded, and cut into chunks

⅓ cup loosely packed fresh basil leaves

½ cup fresh mint leaves

Greek sea salt to taste

1 large ripe avocado

1½ cups plain Greek yogurt (preferably whole-milk)

4 tablespoons extra-virgin Greek olive oil

2 to 3 tablespoons fresh strained lemon juice

1 scant teaspoon ground cumin

Freshly ground black pepper

1 cup ice water

Place the spring onions, garlic, cucumber, and herbs in the bowl of a food processor and pulse on and off with a bit of salt until everything is pureed to a mealy pulp. Score and remove the pulp from the avocado and place that in the food processor bowl, too. Pulse until creamy.

Add the yogurt, olive oil, lemon juice, cumin, and pepper. Pulse until smooth and creamy. Add the ice water and pulse to combine. Chill the soup for at least 1 hour before serving. If the soup is too thick at that point, dilute it with a bit more ice water and adjust the seasonings to taste.

USING YOGURT IN THE KITCHEN
In the Eastern Mediterranean, yogurt is enjoyed at breakfast, lunch, and dinner, in various interesting ways, both sweet and savory. It is often used as a dip or dressing and as the main ingredient in many marinades. Yogurt replaces mayonnaise as a sandwich spread, adds spring and moisture to cakes and homemade phyllo pastry, and stars in countless desserts and drinks.

yogurt cucumber soup

WITH WALNUTS

Throughout the Eastern Mediterranean, yogurt is a basic ingredient, the use of which dates back thousands of years. Fermented dairy has always been an important source of nourishment in this part of the world. Some of these soups, such as the Armenian *Spas*, contain cooked wheat berries and are served hot. Others, like Turkish and Greek *tarator* and *taratori*, respectively, are meant to be refreshing meals on hot days. You can experiment with your own additions to this nourishing, cooling soup. It's a great dinner party dish that can be made ahead and served chilled, garnished elegantly with whatever you like.

MAKES 6 SERVINGS

2 large seedless organic cucumbers

2 cups Greek yogurt

Water as needed or desired

2 to 3 garlic cloves to taste, squeezed through a garlic press

3 tablespoons finely ground walnuts

1 small bunch fresh dill or mint, very finely chopped

Sea salt to taste

2 to 4 tablespoons extra-virgin Greek olive oil, as needed

2 to 3 teaspoons pomegranate molasses (optional)

Mint or dill oil (optional) (see Note)

Wash and dry the cucumbers, leaving their skin intact and trimming their ends. Cut the cucumbers in half lengthwise, then into thin strips, and finally into a fine dice, then set them aside.

Transfer the yogurt to a large bowl and whisk with enough water to reach the consistency desired for soup. You can make it as thick or thin as you like.

Add diced cucumber, minced garlic, walnuts, and dill and stir gently to combine. Season to taste with salt. Swirl in about 2 to 4 tablespoons of olive oil, as desired. Chill the soup, covered, for 3 hours.

Serve cold, drizzled with a thin thread of pomegranate syrup and, if you'd like, mint or dill oil.

NOTE: To make the dill or mint oil, or any herb-infused oil, warm a small bunch of trimmed fresh herbs in a small pot in a cup of good Greek olive oil. This will only take a few minutes. Then, transfer the warm oil to a jar and let it stand for at least 24 hours before using. You can strain the oil into a glass bottle with a pouring nozzle for easier drizzling.

greek salad gazpacho

I really try hard not to let food go to waste, but I often have leftover Greek salad in the summer. With a little embellishment, nothing makes a better gazpacho! You can literally puree leftover Greek salad in a blender or food processor at high speed or make it from scratch, as in this recipe!

MAKES 6 SERVINGS

FOR THE KALAMATA CROUTONS

2 1-inch (2½-cm) slices day-old rye or whole-grain bread, cut into 1-inch (2½-cm) cubes

2 tablespoons kalamata olive paste

2 tablespoons extra-virgin Greek olive oil

FOR THE SOUP

8 large firm, ripe tomatoes, coarsely chopped

2 large green bell peppers, seeded and coarsely chopped

1 fresh green or red chili pepper, seeded and coarsely chopped

1 large red onion, coarsely chopped

1 large seedless cucumber, unpeeled and coarsely chopped

2 garlic cloves, minced

1 tablespoon chopped fresh oregano

1½ cups fresh or good-quality tomato juice

3 tablespoons extra-virgin Greek olive oil, plus a little for oiling the pan

2 tablespoons fresh strained lemon juice

Greek sea salt and white pepper to taste

Preheat the oven to 325°F (160°C). Lightly oil a small sheet pan. In a small bowl, toss the cubed bread, kalamata olive paste, and olive oil together and bake for about 25 minutes, or until crisped. Remove and cool.

Prepare the soup: Puree the tomatoes, peppers, onion, cucumber, and garlic in a food processor. Add the oregano and pulse to combine. Remove and pour into a large bowl. Stir in the tomato juice, olive oil, and lemon juice. Season with salt and pepper and chill for at least 2 hours or up to 6.

Serve in individual bowls, and divide the olive croutons evenly among each bowl.

WASTE NOT, WANT NOT!

The Mediterranean diet is many things, but more than anything, it's a road map for how not to waste food! Turning stale leftover bread into delicious dishes is an age-old tradition that spans the region's many different cuisines. Crostini, bruschetta, Greek bread-based dips like *skordalia*, and more are all ways in which prudent cooks made use of leftover bread. Gazpacho is one such recipe, too! This one crosses boundaries: it has a Spanish soul and a Greek heart!

easy
beans

FOR HEALTH & FLAVOR

Eat beans and live longer. That's become a mantra of sorts among proponents of Blue-Zone eating. Indeed, one of the many common threads people in the Blue Zones share is an embrace of beans as a seminal—sometimes daily—food. National Geographic fellow Dan Buettner created the term Blue Zones to connote the places around the globe where longevity is high. He says that eating a cup of beans a day will prolong your life by four years.

Beans certainly inform the regular diet of many Ikarians, who enjoy them in soups, stews, salads, casseroles, and as purees such as fava (page 31). Beans appear throughout the recipes in this book, but in this chapter, they are the focus of the main course recipes.

Beans are pretty much a perfect food. They are an excellent source of plant-based protein, vitamins, minerals, complex carbs, and fiber. They are very low in fat and have almost no sodium. Dried beans do take a little time and effort to prepare, which is done by soaking and boiling. Low-sodium, good-quality, and preferably organic canned beans are fine by my book, too, especially since most of us are happy to save a little time in the kitchen.

Every bowl of beans is a bowl of goodness. The fiber, protein, and slowly digested complex carbs in beans help keep us sated for hours. Indeed, there is a lot of evidence that eating beans on a regular basis is a surefire way to maintain a healthy weight.

Bean consumption helps heart health by lowering cholesterol because beans are rich in soluble fiber, which attaches to cholesterol particles and flushes them out of the body. If you reduce or eliminate your intake of meat and substitute beans, you will get an added bonus by eliminating or reducing one of the greatest sources of saturated fats. Beans are also palliative when it comes to managing and even preventing type 2 diabetes because the combination of high-quality carbohydrates, lean protein, and that soluble fiber helps to stabilize our body's blood sugar levels and keeps hunger in check.

Beans are ancient, and their consumption in the Eastern Mediterranean has been in evidence since prehistoric times. That staying power alone is enough to help us realize the importance of beans in the Mediterranean diet. Mostly, though, beans are easy to cook, extraordinarily versatile, and delicious. Like almost everything in these pages, the recipes that follow are inspired by a way of eating that has been time-tested and tweaked for modern cooks!

warm lentils

WITH PARSLEY & CRUMBLED NUTS

I like to think of this dish as almost a kind of tabbouleh (but without the grain) because of the abundance of parsley that gets tossed in with the lentils. It's a great dish to serve either warm or at room temperature. Lentils are one of the oldest cultivated pulses in the Eastern Mediterranean and are high up on the list of Ikarian longevity ingredients that carry over to kitchens anywhere.

MAKES 4 SERVINGS

½ pound (225 g) small green or brown lentils

Salt to taste

1½ cups finely chopped fresh flat-leaf parsley

1 medium ripe tomato, seeds removed and diced

1 medium green bell pepper, seeds removed and coarsely chopped

1 large red or yellow onion, coarsely chopped (about 1 cup)

2 scallions, trimmed and washed, cut into thin rounds

1 large garlic clove, peeled and minced

¼ cup extra-virgin Greek olive oil

2 to 4 tablespoons red wine vinegar

Greek sea salt to taste

⅓ cup coarsely ground hazelnuts, cashews, or walnuts

Rinse and drain the lentils. Place them in a large pot covered with about 2 inches (5 cm) of water and bring to a boil. Season with salt. Simmer over gentle heat, uncovered, for 20 to 25 minutes, until the lentils are tender but al dente. As they simmer, skim the foam from the surface. Drain.

In a large serving bowl, combine the lentils with the chopped parsley, diced tomato, pepper, onion, scallion, and garlic. In a separate small bowl, whisk together the olive oil, vinegar, and a pinch of sea salt. Pour the dressing over the lentils, toss everything together gently, top with the ground nuts, and serve.

lentils

WITH CARROTS & CARROT TOP-FETA PESTO

Lentils are my personal go-to feel-good food: satisfying, packed with nutrition, and versatile. I cook them in everything from salads to soups and stews. This recipe falls somewhere in between a salad and a stew, but it's what goes on top and is mixed into the lentils that makes this dish so interesting: carrot tops.

In Ikaria, we eat slightly bitter, antioxidant-packed, lacy carrot greens in savory pies and salads, and sometimes toss them into vegetable soups. They're a good source of vitamins A and C; are rich in iron, calcium, and fiber; have zero fat; and contain a long list of other beneficial nutrients. Bones, eyes, circulation, kidneys, and digestion all benefit from the consumption of carrot greens, so next time you go to the greengrocer, make sure you bring home the whole carrot and use it all!

MAKES 6 SERVINGS

2 tablespoons extra-virgin Greek olive oil, plus more for drizzling into the lentils

1 large red onion, finely chopped

2 large carrots, green tops separated and set aside, carrots pared and cut into a ¼-inch dice

1 garlic clove, minced

2 cups small brown lentils, rinsed and drained

1 tablespoon tomato paste

6 to 8 cups water or vegetable stock

1 large bay leaf

Sea salt to taste

1 tablespoon balsamic vinegar

1 to 2 teaspoons *petimezi* (grape molasses) to taste (optional)

FOR THE PESTO

Green tops from the 2 carrots, leaves only, about 1 cup chopped

1 cup chopped and trimmed baby spinach

½ cup chopped fresh basil

2 to 3 garlic cloves, chopped

½ cup extra-virgin Greek olive oil

½ cup toasted pine nuts, unsalted cashews, or blanched almonds

2 tablespoons crumbled Greek feta

Make the lentils: Heat the olive oil in a large wide pot over medium heat and cook the onion and carrots until slightly caramelized, about 15 minutes. Stir in the garlic and cook for a minute or so to soften.

Add the lentils and toss to coat in the olive oil. Add the tomato paste and stir. Add 6 cups of the liquid and the bay leaf, bring the mixture to a simmer, and cook, slightly covered, until the lentils are tender and have absorbed the water or stock. Add more liquid as needed while the lentils are cooking to keep them moist but not soupy. Season to taste with sea salt and stir in the balsamic vinegar and *petimezi*. The lentils will need about 30 to 40 minutes to cook.

While the lentils are simmering, make the pesto: Chop the carrot leaves and add them to the bowl of a food processor together with the spinach, basil, and garlic. Pulse on and off a few times to combine. Add the olive oil and pine nuts, almonds, or cashews, and pulse on and off until the mixture is a thick paste. Add the feta and pulse to combine.

Pour the lentils into individual bowls, swirl in the pesto, and serve.

white bean stew

WITH EGGPLANT, TOMATO & FETA

Beans are one of the healthiest plant-based foods in the world and a seminal ingredient in the Ikaria longevity diet. I only recently joined the canned bean bandwagon because it never seemed like too much trouble to me to soak my beans overnight and then just boil them for whatever recipe I was preparing. But I understand the desire for convenience, and there are certainly plenty of great canned beans. Look for organic and low sodium if possible. This simple dish is one of many ways in which we combine beans and pulses with vegetables in the Greek kitchen.

MAKES 4 SERVINGS

4 tablespoons extra-virgin Greek olive oil, or more as needed

1 medium red onion, chopped

2 celery stalks, chopped

Greek sea salt to taste

2 garlic cloves, finely chopped

2 medium eggplants, trimmed and cut into 1-inch (2½-cm) cubes

Freshly ground black pepper to taste

2 cups plum tomatoes, drained and chopped

2 (15-ounce / 425 g) cans good-quality cannellini beans, rinsed and drained

1 teaspoon dried Greek oregano

2 tablespoons chopped fresh flat-leaf parsley

2 tablespoons crumbled Greek feta or coarsely grated cashew-milk cheddar

Heat 2 tablespoons of olive oil in a large wide pot or deep frying pan over medium heat and cook the onion and celery until translucent and lightly browned, about 10 minutes. Season with a pinch of salt while cooking. Stir in the garlic and cook, stirring, to soften for about a minute. Remove the onion–celery–garlic mixture to a plate until ready to use and replenish the olive oil with an additional 2 tablespoons.

Add the eggplant cubes to the pan, raise the heat a little, and cook, stirring, until the cubes are lightly browned. Add the onion–celery–garlic mixture back to the pan. Pour in the tomatoes. Season to taste with additional salt and a little black pepper, and let the mixture simmer for about 8 minutes, or until the eggplant is soft.

Add the drained beans to the pot, season with oregano, and cook all together for about 15 minutes, or until everything is tender. Just before removing from heat, stir in the parsley. Serve, drizzled with additional olive oil if desired, and topped with the crumbled feta or cashew-milk cheddar.

lemony giant beans

WITH MUSTARD & DILL

Giant beans—gigantes—are one of the great ingredients of the Greek kitchen, despite their American provenance! All white beans are New World crops. Giant beans are cultivated in a few specific parts of Greece, mostly in the high-altitude areas around Prespes in Macedonia, and in Feneo, a beautiful mountainous region in the northwest Peloponnese. Gigantes are very versatile and make for great soups, casseroles, and even purees. You can substitute butter beans for them in most recipes.

MAKES 6 TO 8 SERVINGS

1 pound (½ kilo) dried giant beans

2 leeks, trimmed and chopped

5 large garlic cloves, minced

⅔ cup extra-virgin Greek olive oil

1 cup dry white wine

6 fresh thyme sprigs

2 bay leaves

Sea salt and freshly ground black pepper to taste

Fresh strained juice of 1 lemon, or more to taste

1 tablespoon Dijon mustard

1 small bunch fresh dill, stems removed, feathery leaves snipped

Soak the giant beans overnight or for at least 8 hours in a large pot with enough water to cover by about 3 inches.

Drain, then fill the pot again with enough cold water to cover the beans by about 2 inches. Bring to a boil over medium-high heat, then reduce the heat to low. Partially cover the pot and simmer the beans for about 1 to 1½ hours, until al dente. Preheat the oven to 350°F (175°C). Drain the beans and reserve their cooking liquid.

Place the beans, leeks, garlic, ⅓ cup of the olive oil, white wine, thyme, and bay leaves in an ovenproof glass or ceramic casserole or baking dish and stir to combine. Add enough of the bean cooking liquid to come just below the surface of the beans. Cover the baking dish and bake the beans for about an hour, or until tender and buttery but still retaining their shape. About halfway through cooking, season to taste with salt and pepper and continue baking, covered. The beans should have absorbed most of the liquid by the end of the baking time.

Whisk together the lemon juice, mustard, and remaining olive oil. Remove the beans from the oven and remove and discard the bay leaves and thyme sprigs. Gently stir the lemon-mustard mixture and snipped dill into the beans and serve hot, warm, or at room temperature.

LUPINI BEANS

Almost all the recipes that call for larger beans such as giant beans and fava beans in this chapter can be replaced with lupini beans. Lupins, or lupini, as they're more commonly known, are a true Ikarian and Mediterranean diet superfood. They are among the most ancient cultivated beans in the Mediterranean. They grow wild all over the north side of Ikaria, and in the spring, their beautiful purple flowers flutter atop stems sturdy enough to hold the fat, fuzzy pods below, where the beans are.

Lupins were once a major food among Ikarians and others throughout Greece. Like soy—so much of which is genetically modified— they are an incredible source of plant protein, but they contain almost no starch, which makes them a great option for people watching their glycemic index.

Lupins have a high alkaloid content, which means they need to be processed and debittered before they are edible. In Greece, you can still see netted bags of lupinis tied to twigs in the sea, the saltwater doing what a brine would otherwise do: ridding the beans of their bitterness. They're then dried. Lupins are a rich source of fiber and contain generous amounts of manganese, copper, magnesium, phosphorus, potassium, and zinc.

You can find them in several forms: dried, brined, and vacuum-packed. The dried beans need to be soaked as you would, say, giant beans, dried favas, or limas; the vacuum-packed beans are ready to cook; and the brined lupins need to be rinsed well to rid them of excess sodium before adding them to recipes. They're also pretty much ready to eat, so you will need to adjust cooking times.

caramelized giant beans

WITH TURMERIC, FENNEL & ROMAINE

Renditions of this recipe are sometimes referred to as gigantes (giant beans) fricassee, a contemporary take on a Greek classic that usually involves pork, chicken, lamb, or fish and lettuce or other leafy greens in a lemony sauce. This rendition is surprisingly elegant, even though it calls for simple, everyday ingredients. You can substitute butter beans for the giant beans.

MAKES 6 TO 8 SERVINGS

1 pound (½ kilo) dried giant beans

½ cup extra-virgin Greek olive oil

6 scallions, trimmed

1 large fennel bulb, coarsely chopped

1 heaping teaspoon ground turmeric

2 heads romaine lettuce, trimmed and washed thoroughly

Fresh strained juice of 1 large lemon

1 tablespoon Greek pine honey

Sea salt and freshly ground black pepper to taste

1 small bunch fresh mint, leaves only, chopped

2 tablespoons chopped fresh oregano or marjoram

Soak the giant beans overnight or for at least 8 hours in a large pot with enough water to cover by about 3 inches.

Drain, then fill the pot again with enough water to cover by about 2 inches and bring to a boil. Simmer the beans partially covered, skimming the foam off the surface of the water now and then, until the beans are tender, about 1 to 1½ hours.

While the beans are simmering, heat 2 tablespoons of olive oil in a large wide pot and cook the scallions and fennel until translucent and soft, about 7 to 8 minutes over medium-low heat, stirring occasionally. Stir in the turmeric and cook for about 30 seconds.

Halve the lettuce leaves lengthwise and then cut them across into ½-inch-wide ribbons. Add the lettuce to the onion mixture. Cover and cook for a few minutes until the lettuce is wilted. Stir all together and set aside.

When the beans are cooked, drain them and reserve 2 cups of their cooking liquid to use as needed. Add the cooked beans to the lettuce mixture. Whisk together the lemon juice, remaining olive oil, honey, and a cup of the bean liquid and stir this into the bean and lettuce mixture. Season generously with salt and pepper. Set the heat to low and cook for about 6 to 8 minutes for everything to meld together. Stir in the mint and marjoram or oregano and serve.

main course giant bean greek salad

I made this recipe for an episode in season 4 of the *My Greek Table* PBS series about the art scene in Athens, in which we planned a dinner party for a group of artists and gallery owners at my daughter's art space in Athens. It was inspired by an old recipe for Ikarian-style potato salad, which is basically a warm potato salad with most of the ingredients of a Greek salad mixed in. Instead of potatoes, I made it with giant beans. The recipe calls for either capers or a popular pickled green called sea fennel or rock samphire, which grows wild along both coasts of the Atlantic. It's particularly esteemed on Ikaria, and we collect it in the spring when the leaves are young and tender. This salad is pretty to look at and also chock-full of nutrition, not only from the beans and fresh vegetables but also the probiotics of olives and capers or samphire, which are naturally fermented and provide a wealth of vitamins, minerals, antioxidants, and delicious acidity!

MAKES 6 TO 8 SERVINGS

2 cups dry giant beans

3 large firm, ripe tomatoes

1 large seedless cucumber

2 green bell peppers, cap and seeds removed

1 large red onion, peeled

12 Greek olives of choice (kalamatas, wrinkled black, green)

2 tablespoons drained capers or sea fennel, as desired

2 large pinches dried Greek oregano

6 tablespoons extra-virgin Greek olive oil

Greek sea salt to taste

½ cup crumbled Greek feta, or more to taste

6 to 8 pickled pepperoncini peppers

Place the beans in a large bowl or pot of cold tap water and let them soak overnight or for about 8 hours. Drain the giant beans and place in a medium saucepan with fresh water. Bring to a boil and simmer over medium heat, partially covered, for about 1 to 1½ hours, or until tender but al dente. Skim the foam off the surface of the beans while they simmer. Drain and transfer to a mixing or serving bowl.

Core and halve the tomatoes. Cut into wedges or chunks. Place in a salad bowl. Remove the cucumber ends and cut the cucumber in half lengthwise and then into ½-inch (1¼-cm) half-moon-shaped pieces. Add to the tomatoes. Cut the bell pepper in half and then into ¼-inch strips. Cut the onion in half and then into slices about ⅛-inch thick. Place in the salad bowl with the beans and other vegetables. Add the olives and capers or sea fennel. Add the oregano and olive oil, toss gently, taste for salt, and adjust the seasoning if needed. Sprinkle the feta over the salad, garnish with the pepperoncini, and serve.

red beans

WITH HOT PEPPER FLAKES & FRESH HERBS

There's a debate between dried versus canned beans and which are better for you. Dried beans are definitely more nutritionally dense and taste richer and fresher. But most require soaking, which has become an apparent inconvenience to many people. Canned beans are a close second in terms of nutrition, and I use them a lot. It's really important to drain and rinse them very well. Canned beans are higher in sodium than dried, and since most of the salt is in the liquid, draining and rinsing will cut down on salt. Look for organic, low-sodium beans if you can.

You can serve this simple recipe over a bowl of brown rice or quinoa to create a meal that is nutritionally whole and chock-full of plant-based protein. It's delicious with a side of Greek yogurt or feta, too!

MAKES 2 SERVINGS

3 tablespoons
fresh lemon juice

2 teaspoons Dijon mustard

½ cup dry white wine

3 garlic cloves, minced

6 tablespoons extra-virgin
Greek olive oil

1 (15-ounce / 425 g) can
kidney or borlotti beans,
rinsed and drained

Greek sea salt to taste

⅓ cup fresh oregano
or marjoram, leaves only,
chopped

½ cup
chopped fresh flat-leaf parsley

½ teaspoon crushed red
pepper flakes, or more to
taste

Whisk together the lemon juice, mustard, wine, garlic, and half the olive oil in a medium bowl. Toss the beans into the mixture. Cover and let stand in the refrigerator for 20 minutes.

Transfer the beans and marinade to a large saucepan and bring to a simmer. Cook uncovered for a few minutes, until the alcohol in the wine cooks off. Adjust the taste with a little salt. Drizzle in the remaining olive oil and mix in the herbs and red pepper flakes.

Serve with a side of Greek yogurt or a small piece of feta, if desired.

spicy fava beans braised in red wine

Fava beans, or broad beans, as they are also known, have a very special place in the Greek diet, being both revered and feared. Rich in folate, antioxidants, and many minerals, including iron, manganese, and copper, fava beans are excellent for bone health and as an immune booster. They're a rich source of plant protein. But they are feared because they can be detrimental, even lethal, to anyone lacking the enzyme that enables them to digest the beans. They were prohibited, as far back as the 6th century BCE, by one of the most famed vegetarians of the ancient world, the father of geometry, Pythagoras, who forbade his followers from consuming them.

Cleaning the dried beans can be a little tricky. In Greece, we generally soak them and remove the black "eye" on the side of the bean, but we don't usually bother removing the entire rather leathery skin on the bean. They're definitely more delicate when it is removed, however.

MAKES 4 TO 6 SERVINGS

2 cups dried fava beans

½ cup extra-virgin Greek olive oil

2 red onions, chopped

6 garlic cloves, minced

2 bay leaves

1 small fresh or dried red chili pepper or ½ teaspoon dried chili flakes, or more to taste

1 cup chopped canned or fresh plum tomatoes

½ cup dry red wine

Salt and freshly ground black pepper to taste

1 tablespoon balsamic vinegar

½ cup chopped fresh mint

Soak the dried favas overnight or for at least 8 hours. Drain, then use a sharp paring knife to remove the black "eye" on the side of the bean. Slip off the skins.

Heat half the olive oil in a large wide pot over medium heat and sauté the onion until soft and translucent, about 8 to 10 minutes, stirring. Add the garlic, swirl it around in the pan for a minute or so, and then add the beans, bay leaves, and chili pepper, tossing to coat everything in the oil.

Add the tomatoes, raise the heat to high, and add the red wine. Let the alcohol cook off for a few minutes, then lower the heat to a simmer. Keep the lid on the pan ajar and simmer the beans until they are tender and the texture is thick and luscious, about 45 minutes. About 10 minutes before removing from heat, season with salt and pepper and stir in the vinegar and mint. Right at the end, when the dish comes off the heat, stir in the remaining olive oil.

dried fava stew

WITH ONIONS, CUMIN & MINT

The innate goodness of traditional recipes in this part of the world never ceases to amaze me. This dish, a traditional one on the island of Crete, where Greek broad beans grow and flourish high up on the Lasithi plain, speaks tomes about the simplicity of Greek island cooking—Ikaria, of course, included. But it also speaks to the bold flavors and incidental healthfulness achieved with the generous use of a few favorite spices and herbs, cumin and mint, in the case of these ancient beans.

Cumin is often used as a pickling spice, for example, because of its antibacterial qualities. Among its many other virtues, empiric knowledge to people around the Eastern Mediterranean, Middle East, and India, and with which science is finally catching up, is its bounty of flavonoids, more of those life-enhancing antioxidants that are a key to health. Mint, too, is a great source of antioxidants, with countless other good things on its side, like its antiviral and antibacterial qualities. Including this duet, so Greek and so simple, in something as humble as a bowl of beans adds health and flavor to the umpteenth power!

MAKES 6 SERVINGS

1 pound (½ kilo) dried fava beans, picked over and rinsed

¾ cup extra-virgin Greek olive oil

2 large red onions, finely chopped

2 garlic cloves, minced

1 heaping teaspoon ground cumin

1½ cups canned chopped plum tomatoes

2 bay leaves

½ cup dry red wine

Salt and freshly ground black pepper to taste

1 to 2 tablespoons balsamic vinegar

1 cup chopped fresh mint

Soak the beans in ample water for 8 hours or overnight. Drain, then use a sharp knife to remove the leathery shells and black "eye" on the side of the beans. Place the favas in a large pot with enough water to cover by about 2 inches, bring to a boil, cook for 10 minutes, and drain. Wipe the pot dry.

Use the same pot to heat half the olive oil over medium-low heat and cook the onions for about 8 minutes, or until translucent. Stir in the garlic. Add the cumin and stir to combine. Add the beans back to the pot. Next, pour in the tomatoes, add the bay leaves, and bring to a simmer over medium heat. Add the red wine and enough water to come just below the surface of the beans. Simmer over low heat partially covered, until the beans are tender, about an hour. There should be very little liquid left in the pot. Remove the bay leaves. Season to taste with salt and pepper and stir in the balsamic vinegar, mint, and remaining olive oil. Serve.

lemony fresh fava beans

WITH ARTICHOKES, TAHINI & YOGURT

This recipe speaks the language of the Mediterranean diet! Fresh favas are one of the great harbingers of spring, and they are savored throughout the Mediterranean. In Greece, we cook them in lemony stews with artichokes or peas and dill or fennel. Sometimes, they're served with a dollop of tangy, thick Greek yogurt, too. This recipe takes some hints from that ingredient, but I love the fresh beans with tahini, too, one of the oldest and most nutritious foods in the Eastern Mediterranean. I highly recommend searching out dark tahini from unhulled sesame seeds. It's even more packed with nutrients and has a deep, nutty flavor that marries beautifully with the grassy freshness of the tender green favas.

MAKES 4 SERVINGS

2 pounds (900 g) shelled fresh fava beans

4 artichoke hearts preserved in olive oil and drained

2 tablespoons capers, rinsed and drained

10 cracked green olives, pitted

½ cup snipped fresh dill or mint

Finely grated zest of 1 lemon

4 tablespoons fresh strained lemon juice

½ teaspoon Greek honey

6 tablespoons extra-virgin Greek olive oil

Sea salt and freshly ground black pepper to taste

⅔ cup plain Greek yogurt

1 tablespoon tahini, preferably from unhulled sesame

½ teaspoon ground cumin, or more to taste

Shell the fava beans and blanch them for 3 minutes in lightly salted water. Remove, drain, and peel off their skins. Place in a mixing bowl.

Cut the artichokes lengthwise into 4 or 6 strips. Add them to the fava beans. Add the capers, olives, dill or mint, and lemon zest.

In a separate mixing bowl, whisk together 2 tablespoons of lemon juice, ½ teaspoon of Greek honey, and 4 tablespoons of olive oil with a little salt and pepper, and pour into fava beans. Allow the mixture to marinate for 10 to 15 minutes at room temperature.

In the meantime, in the same bowl in which you whisked the dressing, whisk together the yogurt, tahini, remaining olive oil and lemon juice, and a pinch of salt, pepper, and cumin. Add this to the fava bean mixture, toss gently, and serve.

black-eyed peas braised

WITH ORANGES, TOMATO & ANISE

I grow *mavromatika*—black-eyed peas—in my summer garden, and we call
them *ambelofasola*, which are essentially fresh runner beans. When fresh, these
delicious, long, thin beans make great salads. They're also great braised with fresh
tomatoes and herbs. But the dried beans are even better. They're so versatile and
easy to cook. Indeed, black-eyed peas are one type of dried beans that don't require
soaking and need a relatively short cooking time. The aromas in this recipe are
among my personal favorites. I love the flavor that slow-cooked unpeeled oranges
impart to many dishes, especially beans. Orange wedges, peel and all, are a great
addition to chickpeas and giant beans, too.

MAKES 6 SERVINGS

1 1-pound (450 g) bag of
black-eyed peas

½ cup extra-virgin olive oil

1 medium red onion, chopped

1 fennel bulb, trimmed and
chopped, feathery fronds set
aside

4 scallions, trimmed and
thinly sliced

2 carrots, peeled and diced

2 garlic cloves, chopped

2 tablespoons tomato paste

1 star anise

2 bay leaves

1 navel orange, preferably
organic, unpeeled and cut into
8 wedges

Sea salt and freshly ground
black pepper to taste

½ cup chopped fresh parsley,
stems removed

1 cup chopped fresh dill fronds

Place the black-eyed peas in a large pot with ample water
and bring to a boil. As soon as they come to a boil, remove
and drain.

In the same pot, heat 4 tablespoons of olive oil and sauté
the onion, fennel, scallions, and carrots until translucent and
lightly browned, about 10 minutes. Stir in the garlic, add the
blanched black-eyed peas, and toss to coat in the olive oil.

Add the tomato paste and stir all together. Add enough
water to come about an inch—not more—above the black-
eyed peas, then add the star anise and bay leaves and squeeze
the orange wedges into the pot. Simmer over low-to-medium
heat until the black-eyed peas are tender, about 40 minutes,
checking the liquid content and adding a little more water
as needed. About 10 minutes before removing from the heat,
season with salt and pepper.

Remove from heat, then remove and discard the bay
leaves and star anise. Stir in the herbs and remaining olive
oil, and serve with the cooked orange wedges.

black beans

WITH SHEET PAN SWEET POTATOES, ROASTED RED PEPPERS & HERBS

Black beans, a Latin American staple, are easy to adapt to the Mediterranean diet. They're a good source of plant-based protein and are among the easiest beans to find canned. They're high in calcium, iron, and fiber. They're also gorgeous to look at and add drama and color to so many dishes. I love to pair them with other colorful ingredients, especially sweet potatoes and roasted red peppers.

MAKES 4 SERVINGS

½ cup extra-virgin Greek olive oil

1 teaspoon sea salt

Freshly ground black pepper, to taste

1 teaspoon cumin seeds

1 teaspoon paprika

2 large sweet potatoes, peeled and cut into ½-inch (1-cm) cubes

2 cups good quality, low-sodium canned black beans, washed, drained, and rinsed, or 2 cups cooked black beans prepared from dried beans, drained

2 roasted red bell peppers, peeled, seeded, and diced

1 medium red onion, minced

1 large garlic clove, minced

⅔ cup finely chopped fresh mint or cilantro

2 tablespoons balsamic vinegar

Sea salt and freshly ground black pepper to taste

Preheat the oven to 400°F (200°C). Layer a baking sheet with parchment paper and set aside.

Mix 4 tablespoons of olive oil, salt, pepper, cumin, and paprika in a mixing bowl, and toss the sweet potatoes in this mixture to coat and season.

Transfer them to the prepared pan, spread in a single layer, and roast for 20 minutes, or until the sweet potatoes are tender and cooked through. It may take a few minutes more or less depending on the size of the potatoes. When the potatoes are tender, remove them from the oven.

Place the drained beans in a large mixing bowl. Add the roasted red peppers, onion, and garlic. Gently toss in the roasted sweet potato cubes and cilantro or mint, and season with remaining olive oil, balsamic vinegar, and additional salt and pepper.

CHICKPEA POWER

It's hard to imagine another legume so closely wedded to so many culinary traditions around the Mediterranean as the chickpea. It's a seminal legume in all the cuisines of the Middle East, where it has been cultivated for ten thousand years. The Byzantines and ancient Greeks both knew it, revered it, and cooked with it. The ancient Greeks likened the shape of its seed to a ram's head, and its original name in ancient Greek denotes that: *erevinthos o kriomorfos*.

It is one of the most versatile legumes; older Ikarians who may have cultivated it in their gardens enjoyed chickpea shoots in the spring—something still savored on the island of Crete.

The legume itself is one of the most nutritious. It's an excellent source of plant-based protein, fiber, B vitamins, and some minerals. It can be ground into a flour and used not only in falafel but also in a traditional hard tack (rusk) called *eptazymo*, also on Crete.

Its earthy flavor and golden color pair beautifully with so many other vegetables; it's delicious with citrus, like lemon juice and orange juice; it's soothing when coupled with small pasta. And it's delicious braised with greens.

Chickpeas are also an easy legume to find canned, so preparing them doesn't take much time and packs a powerhouse for any meal of the day.

chickpea stew
WITH WHOLE WHEAT ORZO & KALE

Recipes for beans and greens or beans and pasta prevail all over the
Mediterranean. They're hearty and healthy and usually fall somewhere between
a soup and a stew. I like to serve this with a very traditional Greek grating cheese
called *myzithra*, which is a sharp whey cheese that's air-dried until it's rock-hard.
You can find it in Greek shops or online. This stew can be made completely vegan,
served with a little grated cashew milk cheese.

MAKES 4 TO 6 SERVINGS

3 tablespoons extra-virgin
olive oil, more for drizzling

1 medium red or yellow onion,
chopped

2 medium carrots, peeled
and chopped

2 celery stalks, chopped

1 fennel bulb, trimmed and
chopped

4 cloves garlic, minced

1 small whole chili pepper
(optional)

6 cups chopped kale

2 cups rinsed and drained
canned chickpeas

1 cup chopped canned plum
tomatoes

2 cups hot vegetable broth
or water

Salt

½ cup whole wheat orzo

Freshly cracked black pepper

½ cup grated Greek
Kefalotyri, dried *myzithra*,
or crumbled feta (optional)

In a large wide pot, heat the olive oil over medium heat. Add
the onion, carrots, celery, and fennel and cook, stirring, until
tender, about 8 minutes. Add the garlic and chili pepper, and
stir for about a minute. Stir in the chopped kale, cover, and
wilt, about 3 minutes.

Add the chickpeas and toss to coat in the oil and vegetable mixture. Stir in the tomatoes and then add the broth
or water. Bring to a boil, season with salt, and add the orzo.
Lower the heat to a simmer, cover the pot, and cook for about
10 minutes, or until the orzo is soft and the mixture thick
and creamy. Remove, adjust seasoning with additional salt
and pepper, and drizzle in the remaining olive oil. Serve, and
garnish, if desired, with the grated cheese.

chickpea stew

WITH HONEY-ROASTED CAULIFLOWER & ROOT VEGETABLES

I embraced the whole sheet-pan craze when my son was still in high school and I discovered it to be such an easy way to cook up so many different things with minimal fuss. Chickpeas are a family favorite in our home. The smoky, spicy-sweet flavors of the vegetables are a delicious addition to the earthy flavor of the chickpeas. Orange is one of the ingredients in my secret arsenal of flavor enhancers, up there with lemon zest and a few other ingredients.

MAKES 6 SERVINGS

FOR THE SHEET-PAN VEGETABLES

Fresh strained juice of 1 orange

½ cup extra-virgin Greek olive oil

2 teaspoons Dijon mustard

1 tablespoon Greek pine honey, or more to taste

2 heaping teaspoons ground cumin

1 pinch freshly grated nutmeg

1 heaping teaspoon turmeric powder

2 teaspoons ground ginger

1 teaspoon smoked paprika

½ teaspoon cayenne or hot paprika, or more to taste

Sea salt and freshly ground black pepper to taste

1 medium head cauliflower, trimmed and cut into small florets

2 carrots, pared, halved lengthwise, and cut into 2-inch pieces

2 large red onions, peeled and quartered

FOR THE CHICKPEAS

2 tablespoons extra-virgin Greek olive oil, plus more for drizzling

1 large red or yellow onion, chopped

4 garlic cloves, chopped

4 cups cooked chickpeas (good-quality canned are fine), rinsed and drained

1 heaping tablespoon tomato paste

1 small seedless orange, preferably organic, cut into 4 wedges

2 fresh rosemary sprigs

2 to 4 cups hot vegetable broth or water, or more as needed

1 tablespoon balsamic vinegar

Preheat the oven to 400°F (200°C). Line a sheet pan with parchment paper.

In a large mixing bowl, whisk together the orange juice, olive oil, mustard, honey, and all the spices including the salt and pepper. Toss the vegetables in this mixture to coat evenly. Spread the vegetables in one layer onto the sheet pan. Roast until tender and lightly charred, about 20 minutes, removing vegetables as they cook to avoid burning them. Set aside to cool and then cut into smaller pieces, a little larger than the chickpeas.

In the meantime, prepare the chickpeas: Heat the olive oil in a large wide pot and sauté the onion until translucent. Stir in the garlic. Add the chickpeas and stir. Stir in the tomato paste. Squeeze the orange wedges into the chickpeas to get out their juice and add the wedges, peel and all, to the pot. Add the rosemary and 2 cups of the hot broth or water. Season to taste with salt and pepper, partially cover the pot, and cook the chickpeas on low for the flavors to meld, about 15 or 20 minutes. If you want the mixture to be thick and creamy, you can mash a handful of chickpeas against the side of the pot.

Add the root vegetables to chickpeas, heat all together for about 5 minutes, stir in the balsamic vinegar, and serve.

garlicky chickpea stew

WITH CARROTS, SUN-DRIED TOMATOES & OLIVES

The Mediterranean lifestyle, spirit, and practical approach to food is in this pot! In a classic Ikarian home, for example, a dish like this would most likely be made in the wintertime when carrots are in season and when an ingredient like sun-dried tomatoes tells the story of summer preserving. Anyone on the island who has an overflow of tomatoes in their garden usually finds ways to preserve them. I, for one, prepare and put up countless sauces, oven-roasted tomatoes, frozen tomato puree, and homemade sun-dried tomatoes, spreading them out on a sheet over a screen, so air can circulate around them. I keep them loosely covered and bring them inside every night, lest the humidity ruin them. Then, when winter comes around and it's bean weather, adding them to a hearty dish is akin to adding a little summer warmth. Olives, the other preserved food here, is a year-round ingredient that I'd venture to say is in the larders of all eleven million Greeks!

MAKES 4 TO 6 SERVINGS

2 tablespoons extra-virgin Greek olive oil

2 medium carrots, peeled and chopped

1 medium yellow onion, chopped

5 cloves garlic, minced

Sea salt and freshly ground black pepper to taste

4 cups good-quality canned or frozen and defrosted chickpeas, drained and rinsed

1 cup diced canned tomatoes, with juices

1 teaspoon dried thyme

1 teaspoon dried Greek oregano

1 sprig fresh rosemary

8 sun-dried tomatoes, reconstituted and chopped

2 cups water or low-sodium vegetable broth, or more as needed

3 tablespoons pitted whole kalamata olives

2 teaspoons fresh lemon juice

Warm the olive oil in a large wide pot over medium-high heat. Add the carrots and onion and cook for about 7 to 8 minutes, until softened and lightly colored. Stir in the garlic and cook for about half a minute, until fragrant. Season with a little salt and pepper.

Stir in the chickpeas, canned diced tomatoes, thyme, oregano, and rosemary. Add the sun-dried tomatoes and the water or broth. Bring the mixture to a boil, then reduce heat to medium-low and simmer for 10 minutes. Add the olives and cook for another 5 to 6 minutes. Stir in the lemon juice, and adjust the seasoning with additional salt and pepper as desired. Drizzle in a little more olive oil and serve.

saffron chickpeas
WITH WHOLE WHEAT ISRAELI COUSCOUS, DRIED FIGS, RAISINS & MINT

There is a tiny, granular, comforting pasta in Greece called *kouskousi.* The closest thing to it is Israeli couscous, sometimes called pearl couscous, also comforting, and all the more so when made with whole wheat for an extra nutty texture. This is a great recipe for luring kids to the bean pot because it is so comforting. Besides olive oil, three other time-tested ancient ingredients inform this dish: saffron, figs, and raisins. The addition of beans or pulses and a grain, whether it's something like Israeli couscous, pasta, rice, or bulgur, transforms the combination into a complete protein.

MAKES 6 SERVINGS

4 tablespoons extra-virgin Greek olive oil

1 large red onion, chopped

1 large carrot, peeled, sliced lengthwise, and then into thin half-moons

1 garlic clove, chopped

1 cup uncooked whole wheat Israeli couscous

3 cups low-sodium vegetable broth

Sea salt and freshly ground black pepper to taste

1 generous pinch Greek saffron, aka Krokos Kozanis

4 cups cooked, good-quality canned chickpeas, rinsed and drained

4 dried figs, preferably kalamata or from Kymi (Evia), chopped

⅓ cup golden raisins or Corinthian currants

½ cup finely chopped fresh mint

Finely grated zest of 1 orange or lemon, as desired

In a large wide pan or deep skillet, heat half the olive oil over medium-high heat. Add the onion and carrot and sauté until softened and lightly colored, about 10 minutes. Add the garlic and swirl it around for about half a minute to release its aroma.

Add the couscous and hot broth. Bring to a simmer over medium heat, season with salt, and stir in the saffron. Cook until the liquid has been absorbed and the couscous is al dente, about 5 minutes.

Stir in the chickpeas and heat through. Stir in the chopped figs and raisins or currants. Stir in the mint, orange or lemon zest, and remaining 2 tablespoons of olive oil. Adjust seasoning with additional salt and pepper and serve.

chickpea–bulgur stew

WITH A RAINBOW OF VEGETABLES

Two ancient Mediterranean ingredients, bulgur and chickpeas, come together in this gently spiced, bright dish. Bulgur—*pligouri* in Greek—is essentially dried, cracked wheat that has been parboiled, which is why it takes so little time to cook. I actually never cook it—I like to soak it instead. When it has absorbed an equal volume of water, it's ready. Bulgur has a chewier consistency than, say, pearl couscous. It is considered a whole grain and is a great source of several minerals, especially manganese, magnesium, and iron. If you want to make this dish gluten-free, substitute unhulled quinoa for the bulgur. Both are nutty and earthy and a great match for the chickpeas, but quinoa has more calories! As for the chickpeas, their long culinary history in the region attests to their nutritional value. Rich in vitamins, minerals, protein, and fiber, chickpeas have a lot going for them!

MAKES 4 TO 6 SERVINGS

1 cup coarse bulgur

4 tablespoons extra-virgin
Greek olive oil

2 medium red or yellow
onions, chopped

1 small fennel bulb, chopped

1 red bell pepper, chopped

1 green bell pepper, chopped

6 garlic cloves, minced

1 tablespoon paprika

2 teaspoons ground ginger

1 teaspoon freshly ground
black pepper

½ teaspoon cayenne pepper

1 quart vegetable broth

1 (28-ounce / 793 g) can
chopped plum tomatoes

1 (15-ounce / 450 g) can
chickpeas, rinsed and drained

1 cup fresh or frozen and
thawed shelled peas

Salt and freshly ground
black pepper

½ cup minced fresh parsley

½ cup snipped fresh dill
or fennel fronds

Place the bulgur in a mixing bowl with 1 cup of water and leave it to soak, covered with a kitchen towel, for about 1½ to 2 hours, until it absorbs all the water and is tender but firm. Set it aside until ready to use. You can do this in the morning and keep it covered with a kitchen towel.

Warm 2 tablespoons of olive oil in a wide pot over medium heat and sauté the onion, fennel bulb, and bell peppers until soft, about 8 minutes. Stir in the garlic, turn it in the pan for about half a minute, then add the paprika, ginger, 1 teaspoon pepper, and cayenne, stirring for about half a minute to release their aromas.

Add the tomatoes, chickpeas, and shelled peas and cook for about 8 to 10 minutes over medium-low heat, until the chickpeas are warmed through and the flavors have melded. Add the bulgur to the pot, season to taste with salt and pepper, and cook for 5 minutes. Stir in the parsley, dill or fennel fronds, and remaining olive oil and serve.

comfort grains

WHOLESOME, HEARTY DELIGHTS

Everywhere you look on Ikaria, you see terraces carved into the mountainsides. Sometimes the terraces are still pronounced, and sometimes they're mere remnants of the past, lines of rocks that have melted back into the earth hinting at past activity. That activity was and is farming, and in the past, the steps were mostly carved for the production of wheat and barley. Carving out steps created arable land that held water. Grains were an essential part of the diet and still are. Indeed, wheat is one of the three pillars of the Mediterranean diet, on par with the olive and its oil, and the vine and all its gifts.

Throughout most of Mediterranean history, grains were consumed whole, unhulled, and minimally processed. It wasn't until the late nineteenth century, with the advent of steel-roller milling, that processed grains became more prevalent. As this milling method spread, the prevailing mindset changed. The whiter the grain, the more luxurious it appeared to be. Up until the 1990s in Greece, and still in some bread bakeries today, the least nutritious breads, made with the whitest flour and thus stripped of most nutrients, are called *polytelias*, or luxury breads!

Wheat and barley are the two most traditional grains in the Ikarian and wider Greek kitchen, and there is luckily a reversed trend now to embrace whole grains. The bran and germ are not only the healthiest part of a wheat shaft; they also imbue wheat products with a delicious nuttiness and great texture. Research consistently shows that consuming whole grains helps us control blood sugar, cholesterol, and inflammation. Whole grains are packed with vitamins, proteins, and trace minerals. When we combine them with vegetables and other plant-based foods, as well as extra-virgin olive oil, we end up with power plates that are delicious, too.

I love pasta, and that is reflected in the many recipes for it in this chapter, all either whole wheat or protein-based, which I have also come to like and cook quite often. Bulgur, another wheat product, is also a favorite, and it appears in a few recipes throughout the book. Chewy, high-fiber, and protein-rich farro is another grain I love, and I offer a recipe for it in the "Tossed" chapter, page 85. I've been experimenting, too, with a new ancient wheat pasta called zea, which is similar to emmer.

It's always fun to experiment with the toppings for pasta dishes, and one of my favorite endeavors is to create sauces that emulate the heartiness and richness of meat sauces but are totally plant-based and natural, meaning not made with meat wannabees like soy meal or laboratory meats. Lentils and chestnuts are both great options, and in this chapter, you'll find two recipes using both.

Other grains that are used as the foundation for main courses in this chapter include rice and quinoa, both as pilafs piled high with vegetables. Quinoa is new to the Greek kitchen, but thanks to its mild, nutty flavor and how easy it is to cook, it adapts beautifully to so many Mediterranean dishes. Rice has long been a part of the food landscape here, and it appears throughout the book, although, admittedly, I like white rice better than brown, so I allowed a little wiggle room when it comes to using it.

vegan wild mushroom orzo "risotto"

WITH SUN-DRIED TOMATOES & CASHEWS

In the spirit of Ikaria, where mushrooms figure very prominently in the winter diet and make for one of several good reasons to head out into the cold with friends, combining exercise, camaraderie, and the anticipation of a social gathering replete with wine, music, and the warmth of a fireplace well lit, I have included a heaping handful of mushroom recipes in this book. This orzo-mushroom mix is sometimes called *kritharoto*, combining the Greek word for orzo, *kritharaki*, with the word *risotto*, for the way the dish is prepared, incrementally adding liquid to the pasta as one does for that Italian classic. I often cook a nonvegan version as well, but I love the idea of making something so satisfying and totally plant-based.

MAKES 4 SERVINGS

2 pounds (900 g) mixed fresh mushrooms, such as button mushrooms, shiitakes, chanterelles, oyster mushrooms, or cepes

1 ounce (28 g) dried porcini mushrooms

⅓ cup extra-virgin Greek olive oil

2 medium red onions, finely chopped

2 green bell peppers, diced

4 garlic cloves chopped

1½ cups whole wheat orzo

⅔ cup dry white wine

4 sun-dried tomatoes

2 to 5 cups hot mushroom or vegetable stock, as needed

1 teaspoon red pepper flakes, or to taste

6 sprigs fresh thyme

1 cup finely ground raw cashews (see Note)

Using a damp kitchen towel, wipe any debris or dirt off the fresh mushrooms. If you're using shiitakes and they're large, cut them in half lengthwise. Cut the oyster mushrooms into ½-inch-wide (1½-cm) strips, using their rippled underside as a guide. Soak the porcini mushrooms in a medium bowl with enough warm water to cover by an inch, and set aside.

Heat the olive oil in a large wide pan over medium heat and cook the onions and peppers until soft. Add the garlic and stir. Gently stir in the fresh mushrooms. Remove the dried porcini from their soaking liquid with a slotted spoon, and strain and reserve their soaking liquid. Add the soaked porcini and their liquid to the pan.

Next, add the orzo, and toss to coat in the oil.

Pour in the wine, and when it comes to a simmer and the alcohol cooks off, after about 5 minutes, stirring all the while, add the chopped sun-dried tomatoes. Add 2 cups of hot stock, red pepper flakes, and thyme. Reduce heat to low and simmer, stirring and adding water or additional stock as needed, until the orzo is cooked and creamy. Stir in the ground cashews and serve.

NOTE: You can replace the ground cashews with ⅔ cup of grated Parmigiano or Greek Kefalograviera cheese.

vegan chickpea pasta

WITH CAULIFLOWER, WALNUTS & ORANGE

I have really come to embrace some of the legume-based pasta that has taken over a large patch of the supermarket pasta shelf. The good ones are nutty and wholesome and leave you feeling sated without the carb-overload feeling that wheat pasta sometimes causes. But in this recipe, it's the topping that is unique. In the Greek kitchen, cauliflower has been a main course vegetable long before anyone ever thought of ricing it as faux mashed potatoes or using it as a pizza crust. There are numerous traditional Greek recipes for stewed cauliflower, the inspiration for this dish.

MAKES 2 TO 4 SERVINGS

1 medium head of cauliflower, trimmed

1 medium orange with rind, preferably organic, washed well

3 tablespoons extra-virgin Greek olive oil or more, as desired

2 medium red onions, coarsely chopped

3 large garlic cloves, finely chopped

½ teaspoon ground cumin, or more to taste

1 scant teaspoon ground turmeric, or more to taste

½ teaspoon curry powder, or more to taste

Salt and freshly ground black pepper to taste

5 sun-dried tomatoes in olive oil, drained and finely chopped

2 sprigs fresh rosemary

½ pound (225 g) chickpea or whole wheat pasta, preferably tagliatelle or noodles

4 tablespoons ground walnuts, lightly toasted

Cut the cauliflower in half from the crown to the base. Place each half flat-side down and cut in half again. Slice the cauliflower into thin pieces to resemble a cross-section of florets. Wash well and drain.

Cut the orange in quarters lengthwise and cut each quarter into small wedges, about ¼-inch (50-mm) thick.

Heat the olive oil in a large deep skillet over medium heat and cook the onion, stirring, until wilted. Stir in the garlic. Add the cauliflower pieces and toss to coat in the oil. Stir in the spices, tossing the cauliflower so it's covered with and yellowed from the turmeric, cumin, and curry. Season with salt and pepper and stir in the orange pieces and chopped sun-dried tomatoes. Add the rosemary. Add about ½ cup of water to the pan. Place the lid over the pan and cook the cauliflower until it is soft but still al dente, about 15 to 20 minutes.

While the cauliflower is cooking, bring a large pot of water to a rolling boil and season generously with salt. Add the pasta and cook according to package directions. Drain.

Toss the pasta with the cauliflower in the pan and serve, garnished with walnuts and a little extra olive oil, if desired.

toasted whole wheat orzo pilaf
WITH PISTACHIOS & CURRANTS

This recipe, adapted from season four of *My Greek Table*, is one of the best Greek pasta recipes I've ever made. There is an umami quality to the combination of toasted orzo, Greek saffron, nuts, currants, and vegetables. A lot of the ingredients are actually what Ikarian cooks would typically use in a rice pilaf or stuffing. I highly recommend that you look for tiny, intensely flavored Aegina pistachios, which are available online and in Greek shops. They are prized for their delicious flavor and crunchy texture, thanks to the unique microclimate of Aegina, an island in the Saronic Gulf where they are cultivated.

MAKES 4 TO 6 SERVINGS

6 cups hot vegetable broth or stock or water

4 tablespoons extra-virgin Greek olive oil

1 large red or yellow onion, chopped

1 large carrot, peeled and diced

2 garlic cloves minced

1½ cups whole wheat orzo pasta, divided

1 pinch Greek Krokos (saffron)

Sea salt to taste

⅔ cup Aegina or other pistachios, shelled and toasted

3 tablespoons pine nuts, toasted

3 to 4 tablespoons Corinthian currants or raisins plumped in warm water

2 tablespoons chopped mint/parsley

In a large pot, simmer 6 cups of hot water or vegetable broth over medium-low heat.

Heat half the olive oil in a large deep frying pan over medium heat and cook the onion and carrot until soft, lightly browned, and glistening, about 8 minutes.

Stir in the garlic. Add half the orzo to the pan and continue to cook until the orzo starts to brown, stirring it frequently to keep it from burning, for about 5 to 6 minutes. Sprinkle the saffron into the toasting orzo and add 1 cup of hot liquid. Stir. Add more hot liquid in half-cup increments until the browned orzo is soft but al dente, about 7 minutes.

Bring a medium pot of water to a rolling boil, add a generous tablespoon of salt, and boil the remaining orzo. Drain, reserving 1 cup of its boiling liquid.

Add the boiled orzo to the toasted orzo mixture in the frying pan and stir together gently to combine. Stir in the toasted nuts, currants or raisins and their soaking liquid, and a few tablespoons (or more as desired) of the reserved pasta water to loosen the orzo a bit and make it creamy. Stir in the mint and/or parsley and serve.

fiber-rich fusilli

WITH GREEK SALAD, LIME & BASIL

This is a go-to after-the-beach pasta recipe I make a lot in Ikaria, especially at the height of summer when the tomatoes are heavy on the vine, bursting with ripeness and flavor. I also love the idea of using iconic Greek recipes like a Greek salad (see the Giant Bean Greek Salad recipe, page 136, and the Greek Salad Gazpacho, page 121) or spanakopita filling (see the Cauliflower Steak Melt with Spanakopita, page 232) and transforming or repurposing them into something else. So this pasta salad, served warm or at room temperature, is basically a toss of whole wheat or protein-based corkscrew-shaped pasta (fusilli) with the ingredients of a Greek salad minus the feta and with a twist of lime—*moscholemono* in Greek—a very refreshing combo! You can switch out the pasta shapes to anything similar in size, like rigatoni or bow ties.

MAKES 4 SERVINGS

10 fresh, firm, ripe plum tomatoes or 3 or 4 Jersey beefsteaks or other summer tomato, ripe, juicy, and firm

1 medium red onion

1 cucumber, preferably organic

1 garlic clove, minced

Sea salt for the pasta and to taste

6 to 8 tablespoons extra-virgin Greek olive oil

½ pound (225 g) fusilli, made from either chickpea or lentil flour

1 lime

⅔ cup pitted kalamata olives, whole or chopped

1 small bunch fresh basil, leaves only, cut into thin strips (chiffonade)

Freshly ground black pepper

Core and cut the tomatoes into quarters lengthwise, and then into chunks or wedges. Cut the onion in half and then into slices about $\frac{1}{8}$-inch thick. Trim the ends off the cucumber, halve lengthwise, and cut into half-moon slices about $\frac{1}{8}$-inch thick. Transfer the vegetables to a large bowl, toss them together with the garlic, a little sea salt, and 2 tablespoons of olive oil and let them macerate for about a half hour for their flavors to meld.

Bring a large pot of water to a rolling boil, salt generously, and boil the pasta according to package directions. Drain and toss with 3 tablespoons of olive oil.

Add the vegetable mixture and juices to the pasta. Zest and mix in the lime, olives, and basil. Cut the zested lime into small wedges and toss that into the pasta as well. Mix in the remaining olive oil. Adjust seasoning with salt and pepper, toss, and serve.

About Bean-Based Pasta

Pasta made from pulses such as lentils, chickpeas, and beans has more protein and fiber than traditional wheat pasta.

Pulse-based pastas are mostly gluten-free, but you should always double-check the package because some brands are a combination of pulse and wheat flours. Most of these pastas can count as a vegetable serving; that's how nutrient-dense they are.

charred vegetables

WITH WHOLE WHEAT PASTA & MUSHROOM STOCK

Our family house is often occupied by a nonstop parade of young people—my kids' friends—whose planned "short" stays typically extend serendipitously well past what most people would consider polite! (Just kidding!) Mama D cooks for them with joy, and a lot of what they like is either quickly slapped on the grill or tossed with pasta. Our garden is usually brimming with an excess of pretty much everything, and consuming its offerings becomes, well, a consuming passion for the months I am on the island. This recipe is a potpourri of all sorts of veggies and a bunch of mushrooms, but it also calls for one of the secret ingredients in my cook's arsenal: mushroom stock.

MAKES 4 TO 6 SERVINGS

1 whole head of garlic

2 large red onions, cut into 8 wedges each

½ cup extra-virgin Greek olive oil, or more as needed

Sea salt and freshly ground black pepper to taste

1 large carrot, pared and sliced on the bias into ⅛-inch ovals

3 green or red bell peppers, seeded and cut into 1-inch (⅔-cm) strips

2 cups string beans (cut into 1½-inch- or 4-cm-long pieces)

10 plum tomatoes, cored and halved lengthwise

4 tablespoons balsamic vinegar

1 large zucchini, trimmed and cut into ¼-inch rounds

1 small eggplant, trimmed and cut into 2-inch (5-cm) cubes

10 large button mushrooms, trimmed and halved

1½ quarts good-quality mushroom stock, preferably organic

12 fresh large basil leaves, cut into a chiffonade (thin ribbons)

6 fresh thyme sprigs, leaves pulled off and minced

6 fresh oregano sprigs, leaves pulled off and minced

4 fresh sage leaves, cut into a chiffonade

1 pound (450 g) whole wheat fusilli or other pasta of choice

Preheat the broiler. Line 2 sheet pans with parchment paper. Using a serrated or chef's knife, cut a slice off the top end of the whole garlic, leaving the cloves slightly exposed. Wrap the garlic in aluminum foil and place it on the bottom of the oven to roast while the vegetables are charring.

In a large mixing bowl, toss the onion wedges with a tablespoon of olive oil and a little sea salt and pepper and place on one side of the sheet pan, leaving room for the rest of the vegetables. Next, in the same bowl, toss the carrot slices with 1 tablespoon of olive oil, salt, and pepper, and strew them next to the onions. Continue with the pepper strips, then the string beans. Place the tomatoes on the sheet pan, cut-side up, after tossing them in a little olive oil, salt, and pepper. These are the tougher (or wetter) vegetables that will take more time than the others to cook under the broiler. Drizzle 2 tablespoons of the balsamic vinegar over the vegetables. Keep an eye on them, tossing gently and neatly as they start to char and broil. Cook until tender but lightly crisped and charred. Remove and set aside.

Toss the remaining vegetables (zucchini, eggplant, and mushrooms) in olive oil, salt, and pepper and strew them on the second sheet. Drizzle with the remaining 2 tablespoons of balsamic vinegar. Place them in the oven, either next to the first sheet pan or on the rack under it, switching places when the first batch of vegetables is ready, and broiling and turning once or twice, until these, too, are charred.

Bring the mushroom stock to a boil—taste it, and add salt as needed to make the pasta palatable. Cook the pasta in the mushroom stock. Drain and reserve about a cup of the cooking liquid to use as needed. Transfer the hot pasta to a mixing bowl.

Toss the hot pasta and charred vegetables and all their juices together in a large mixing bowl. Remove the garlic from the oven and squeeze out the softened pulp into the pasta. Toss with the herbs and serve.

ferry boat spaghetti

WITH SPICED LENTILS

This is my vegan version of the classic Greek spaghetti and ground meat sauce called *makaronia me kima*, or, more prosaically *Vaporisia Makaronia*—Ferry Boat Pasta. The spices and flavorings are the same as in the classic version, especially the telltale use of cinnamon. It makes for a hearty, warming pasta dish that's easy, healthy, and inexpensive to prepare.

MAKES 4 SERVINGS

½ cup extra-virgin Greek olive oil

1 large yellow or red onion, finely chopped

1 large carrot, peeled and finely chopped

2 celery stalks, finely chopped

1 small fennel bulb, finely chopped

4 garlic cloves, minced

1½ cups small brown lentils, rinsed and drained

1 heaping tablespoon tomato paste

3 cups crushed canned tomatoes and their juices

½ cup dry red wine

2 cups water

2 large fresh or dried bay leaves

6 fresh or dried thyme sprigs

4 fresh or dried oregano sprigs

1 cinnamon stick

6 allspice berries

1 generous pinch freshly grated nutmeg

1 pinch cayenne

Greek sea salt to taste

Freshly ground black pepper

1 tablespoon balsamic vinegar

1 pound (450 g) whole wheat spaghetti

½ cup chopped fresh parsley

Heat the olive oil in a large pot over low-to-medium heat and add all the chopped vegetables. Toss to coat in the olive oil. Stir in the garlic. Add the lentils and stir. Add the tomato paste and mix it in to distribute evenly. Cover the pot, reduce the heat to low, and let everything cook together for 5 minutes.

Add crushed tomatoes to the pot. Raise the heat to medium and bring the lentils to a simmer, then add the wine. Bring that to a simmer and cook for 5 minutes to boil off the alcohol. Add enough water to come about $\frac{1}{2}$ an inch or so above the lentils. Add the bay leaves, thyme and oregano sprigs, cinnamon, allspice berries, nutmeg, cayenne, salt, and pepper.

Bring to a boil, then reduce heat to low and simmer, covered, until lentils are tender, about 1 hour. Add more water as necessary.

Stir in the balsamic vinegar for about 10 minutes before removing from heat.

While the lentils are simmering, prepare the spaghetti according to package directions, and time it so that the spaghetti is hot and ready when the sauce is cooked. Serve the lentil sauce over the spaghetti and sprinkle with chopped parsley.

NOTE: You can grate a little cashew-milk cheese over the top and get some of the crunch and fat feel that cheese provides with nuts. I'd be inclined to chop hazelnuts or unsalted cashews and toast them lightly before sprinkling over the lentils and spaghetti.

elegant morels

We call morels *morilia* in Greek, and they are one of the great spring treats for mushroom lovers. Morels have an earthy, nutty flavor and a meaty texture. They're also packed with antioxidants, essential minerals, and vitamins and have some of the highest amounts of vitamin D among all edible mushrooms.

MAKES 2 TO 4 SERVINGS

1 ounce (28 g) dried morels

3 tablespoons extra-virgin Greek olive oil

4 large shallots, finely chopped, or 1 cup chopped red onion

2 garlic cloves, minced

6 sprigs fresh thyme

4 tablespoons sweet sherry, port, or Greek Mavrodafni wine

½ cup unsweetened almond milk

1 cup vegetable or mushroom broth

1 teaspoon cornstarch

1 teaspoon *petimezi*

Sea salt and freshly ground black pepper to taste

12 ounces (340 g) chickpea, lentil, or whole wheat pasta, such as fusilli or rigatoni

2 tablespoons grated Greek Kefalotyri, Parmigiano, or Pecorino Romano or other sharp yellow sheep's-milk cheese, or 2 tablespoons grated cashew-milk sharp vegan cheese (optional)

Soak the morels in a bowl of warm water (about 2 cups) for 15 minutes to soften. Drain and set the softened morels aside for a few minutes. Reserve their soaking liquid and pass it through a fine mesh sieve or coffee filter to catch any debris.

Heat the olive oil in a large wide frying pan over medium heat and cook the shallots until translucent, about 8 minutes, stirring occasionally. Stir in the garlic.

Add the whole morels and thyme, and stir. Add the wine and cook over medium heat for about 3 minutes, until the alcohol burns off.

In a small bowl, whisk together 1 cup of the filtered morel liquid, almond milk, mushroom or vegetable broth, and cornstarch. Add this to the morels. Cook until thickened, about 6 to 8 minutes. Drizzle in the *petimezi* and season to taste with salt and pepper.

Cook the pasta according to package directions, drain, and toss with the morel sauce and grated cheese, if using.

whole wheat pasta WITH MUSHROOMS & CHESTNUTS

I was inspired to create this dish by the hundred-year-old chestnut tree growing in my in-laws' garden on Ikaria and by memories of hauling bags of chestnuts from the island every fall, then arduously boiling, slitting, shelling, and roasting them all winter long. While nuts are an important food in Ikaria's longevity diet and throughout the other Blue Zones, chestnuts have a very special place.

They are unique because, unlike most other nuts, chestnuts are rich in vitamin C. Half a cup of raw chestnuts gives you 35 to 45 percent of your daily intake of vitamin C. They're also packed with antioxidants and minerals like potassium and magnesium, and a diet rich in plants and brimming with antioxidants and minerals is among the longevity secrets of Ikarians and others in the Blue Zones.

MAKES 6 SERVINGS

3 cups cooked and shelled chestnuts, preferably vacuum-packed

2 tablespoons extra-virgin Greek olive oil, plus more for tossing with pasta

2 red onions, chopped

3 garlic cloves, chopped

1 pound (½ kilo) fresh button mushrooms, trimmed and sliced

½ cup dry red wine

Greek sea salt and freshly ground black pepper to taste

3 cups fresh teardrop tomatoes, halved lengthwise

1 tablespoon dried Greek oregano or thyme

1 pound (½ kilo) whole wheat or protein-based linguine or spaghetti

Grated cashew-milk cheddar (optional)

If using vacuum-packed chestnuts, poach them in the vacuum-pack bags for 3 to 5 minutes, or as per package instructions, remove, cool slightly, and open the packets to remove the chestnuts.

Heat a deep, medium-sized skillet over medium heat. Add the olive oil and cook the chopped onions, stirring, for about 7 minutes, until the onions soften and start to brown a little. Stir in the garlic and add the chestnuts.

Add the mushrooms, and toss gently with the mixture. Cook, covered, for about 7 minutes, or until the mushrooms are soft and wilted. Add the red wine, raise heat, bring to a simmer, and cook for a few minutes, for the alcohol to burn off. Season with salt and pepper. Reduce heat, cover, and cook slowly, replenishing the liquid if needed with a little water, for about 10 minutes. Gently stir in the tomatoes and then the oregano or thyme and cook all together for 5 to 8 more minutes, or until everything melds together.

While the sauce mixture is simmering, bring a large pot of water to a rolling boil and add 2 tablespoons of sea salt. Boil the pasta according to package directions. Drain, and save a ½ cup of the cooking liquid. Add this to the simmering sauce mixture. Stir, and remove from heat.

Toss the pasta with 2 tablespoons of olive oil and serve with cashew-milk cheese, if using.

creamy pasta

WITH YOGURT-WALNUT SAUCE

Many years ago, I came across an old recipe from Northern Greece for a Lenten phyllo pie filled with ground walnuts and tomatoes, a mixture that approximated the texture of ground meat. Using walnuts was a brilliant idea, especially as it spoke so eloquently to the simplicity and ingenuity of country cooks, and resulted in a dish that sprung from the land and a specific place. In the landscape of northwestern Ikaria, walnut trees abound, and a beautiful site they are, especially in the spring when the nuts are green and soft in the shell and women still bother to collect them, soaking and processing them for a biblical forty days to leach out bitterness and black liquid, all to make a rare but much-esteemed preserve. There is even a village named Karydies—the Greek word for walnuts is *karydi*! Walnuts are also a common snack and easy meze, and they are appreciated for their sound nutrition.

Nut consumption is an important antiaging secret. In fact, a Harvard study published in August 2021 showed that "even a few handfuls of walnuts per week may help promote longevity, especially among those whose diet quality isn't great to begin with," as written by the lead scientist in this study, Yanping Li from the Harvard T. H. Chan School of Public Health. This easy recipe breathes new life into an old Greek habit and tastes great, too! If I were on Ikaria, I'd make it with *matsi*, a local noodle. Any good flat, long noodle–type pasta works.

MAKES 4 TO 6 SERVINGS

1½ cups walnut halves

2 tablespoons extra-virgin Greek olive oil

1 medium red or yellow onion, very finely chopped

3 garlic cloves, minced

3 large firm, ripe tomatoes, peeled, seeded, and pureed in a food processor, or 2 cups chopped canned tomatoes

1 tablespoon Greek sea salt

1 pound (½ kilo) whole wheat or emmer wheat fettuccine, boiled to al dente in salted water and drained

6 fresh oregano or marjoram sprigs, leaves pulled off and chopped

6 mint sprigs, leaves only, chopped

4 thyme sprigs, leaves pulled off and chopped

Freshly ground black pepper to taste

½ cup plain Greek yogurt or nondairy cashew-milk yogurt

Lightly toast the walnuts in a dry skillet for a few minutes, stirring constantly to keep them from burning. Set aside ½ cup of the toasted walnuts and grind the rest to a coarse, mealy consistency by pulsing on and off in the bowl of a food processor.

Heat the olive oil in a separate large skillet, add the onion, and cook over medium-low heat until very soft and starting to turn golden, about 15 minutes. Add the garlic and stir for a minute or so. Add the pureed fresh or canned tomatoes. Cook for about 8 minutes, until the sauce starts to thicken. Add the toasted, ground walnuts.

Bring about 4 quarts of water to a rolling boil, add a heaping tablespoon of salt, and cook the pasta according to package directions.

While the pasta simmers, continue cooking the sauce, and a couple of minutes before draining the pasta, remove the sauce from the heat and stir in the fresh herbs, salt and pepper to taste, and the yogurt, whisking it in vigorously to combine.

Drain the pasta and reserve a cup of its cooking liquid.

In a large mixing bowl, combine the hot pasta, tomato-walnut sauce, and as much additional pasta water as necessary for the sauce and pasta to be well combined and creamy. Serve garnished with remaining toasted walnut halves.

NOTE: You can make this totally vegan by omitting the yogurt or using a good-quality vegan yogurt in its place.

vegetable spaghetti
WITH TAHINI & SESAME SEEDS

This recipe takes its cue from a few very old Greek pasta recipes tossed with tahini (one of the best plant–based sources of calcium), which were prepared most typically for nursing mothers. It reminds me faintly of one of my favorite non–Greek dishes, cold noodles with sesame sauce!

MAKES 4 TO 6 SERVINGS

1 cup tahini, preferably from unhulled sesame

½ cup extra-virgin Greek olive oil, or more, as needed

2 to 3 tablespoons lemon juice to taste

Greek sea salt to taste

1 pinch cumin

3 garlic cloves, minced

½ cup water

3 cups raw broccoli florets (cut small)

2 medium carrots, peeled and diced

2 medium zucchinis, trimmed and diced

1 large red bell pepper seeded and sliced thinly

3 tablespoons ouzo

Salt to taste

1 pound (450 g) whole wheat or legume-based spaghetti

2 tablespoons sesame or nigella seeds

In the bowl of a food processor, beat together the tahini, 6 tablespoons of olive oil, lemon juice, sea salt, cumin, garlic, and enough water to make a thick, creamy paste.

Heat the 2 tablespoons of olive oil in a large frying pan over medium heat and quickly sauté the broccoli florets. Add the carrots and stir. Add the zucchini and peppers. Raise heat to medium and carefully add the ouzo. Stir all together quickly and gently for about 4 minutes, until al dente. Season to taste with salt. Cover and set aside.

Cook pasta according to the package instructions. Drain and reserve 1 cup of the pasta cooking liquid. Add a little of it to the tahini mixture, processing until smooth. Continue to add a little more, as needed, to create a creamy, smooth sauce.

In a large bowl, toss together the pasta, vegetables, and tahini sauce. Serve garnished with sesame seeds.

saffron leek quinoa pilaf

Quinoa is a great addition for anyone who wants to cut back on meat. A single cup of cooked quinoa has around 8 grams of protein, which is roughly the same protein content as a single egg. It has a nice, meaty texture, which makes it incredibly fulfilling, and it will keep you full for hours.

There are three types of quinoa: white, red, and black. The most common type is white quinoa, which has the most delicate and lightest flavor of the three. It also cooks up the fluffiest. Red quinoa keeps its shape and is nuttier and chewier than white. Black quinoa is a bit sweeter and earthier than the other two types and lends visual drama to recipes because of its striking color.

MAKES 4 SERVINGS

1 cup quinoa, preferably unhulled (see Note)

2 pinches Greek saffron, aka Krokos Kozanis

Greek sea salt to taste

2 large leeks, trimmed, halved lengthwise, and cut into crescents

3 tablespoons extra-virgin Greek olive oil

1 cinnamon stick

3 large garlic cloves, finely chopped

2 cups teardrop tomatoes, halved lengthwise

½ cup dry white or rosé wine

½ cup unsalted pistachios, toasted

½ cup Greek currants or dark raisins

½ cup chopped fresh mint

Freshly ground black pepper to taste

Cook the quinoa according to package directions, adding a generous pinch of saffron and salt to the water. Drain and set aside.

Place the chopped leeks in the bowl of a salad spinner, fill with water, and swish around so that any sand or dirt falls to the bottom. Alternatively, place the chopped leeks in a bowl or basin filled with cold water and swish around to allow any sand or dirt to fall to the bottom. Scoop out into the strainer if using a salad spinner, or into a colander. Discard the water, and repeat the process until the leeks are clean.

Heat the olive oil in a large wide skillet over low heat and add the leeks and cinnamon stick. Cook until the leeks are soft, about 10 to 12 minutes. Stir in the garlic. Add the tomatoes, shake the pan back and forth to combine, and cook for 5 minutes over medium-high heat until the tomatoes start to crinkle. Add the wine, and when it steams off, stir in the pistachios, currants or raisins, and salt to taste. Add the cooked, drained quinoa and the mint. Toss gently in the pan so that everything is combined. Taste for salt and pepper and adjust seasoning if needed. Remove from heat and serve.

NOTE: This dish looks great if you mix white and red (unhulled) quinoa together!

cabbage rice & beans

Lahanorizo, or cabbage rice, is one of the simplest Greek dishes, something to make on chilly winter weeknights when cabbage is in season. In traditional recipes, beans aren't usually added to the mixture, but I like the heartiness they contribute, and they make this an easy vegan main course.

MAKES 4 SERVINGS

¼ cup extra-virgin Greek olive oil

1 large leek, trimmed, washed, and chopped

1 large red onion, chopped

2 celery ribs, finely chopped

3 garlic cloves, minced

1 cabbage head, about a pound (450 g), trimmed and coarsely shredded

1 scant teaspoon smoked paprika or Aleppo pepper

1 tablespoon tomato paste

⅔ cup short-grain rice, such as Greek glacé or sushi rice

⅔ cup dry white wine

2 to 4 cups vegetable stock or broth, as needed

1 cup cooked cannellini beans (good-quality canned are fine)

Sea salt and freshly ground black pepper to taste

Finely grated zest of 1 lemon, preferably organic

1 small bunch parsley, leaves only, chopped

Heat the olive oil in a large wide pot over medium heat and cook the leek and onion until soft, lightly colored, and translucent, about 8 minutes, stirring. Stir in the finely chopped celery and cook for about 2 to 3 minutes, until softened. Add the garlic, give it a swirl, and then add the coarsely shredded cabbage, in batches if necessary, until it loses volume and all of it is in the pan. Cover and steam in its own juices for 2 to 3 minutes.

Stir in the paprika, then stir in the tomato paste. Cook all together, stirring, for a minute or so.

Add the rice, stir it into the vegetables, and pour in ⅔ cup of wine. When it steams up and cooks off, add 1 cup of vegetable stock. Lower the heat and simmer, adding more stock as needed, in ½-cup increments, until the rice is tender and the mixture creamy. About 10 minutes before removing from heat, stir in the beans. Season to taste with salt and pepper, add the lemon zest and parsley, and serve.

longevity greens rice

Ikarians enjoy small handheld pies called *pitarakia*, which have a filling of up to twenty different greens and herbs, onions, leeks, and olive oil, all depending on what is in season. I've taken the idea and turned it into the kind of rice dish that is so beloved both in Ikaria and throughout Greece, a comforting, soft dish silky with olive oil and sprightly with all the nutrition that so many greens and herbs impart. This is a version of the category of dishes called *ladera*, "of oil," the oil, of course, being the golden green juice of the olive. You can create your own combination of greens and herbs, too, with such ingredients as sweet sorrel, beet greens, and other sweet greens (see *Horta*, page 76).

MAKES 4 TO 6 SERVINGS

1 pound (½ kilo) Swiss or rainbow chard

½ pound (½ kilo) spinach, trimmed

⅔ cup extra-virgin Greek olive oil

1 large leek, trimmed, washed, and finely chopped

1 large red onion, finely chopped

1 medium fennel bulb, trimmed and finely chopped

2 carrots, peeled and chopped

3 garlic cloves, finely chopped

1 cup long- or medium-grain rice or parboiled brown rice

Salt and freshly ground black pepper to taste

2 cups vegetable stock, or more as needed

½ cup chopped fresh dill

½ cup chopped fresh mint

½ cup chopped fresh chervil (optional)

½ cup chopped fresh flat-leaf parsley

3 tablespoons chopped fresh oregano

Strained juice of 1 lemon

Feta cheese or plain Greek yogurt, for serving (optional)

Trim the chard and spinach, separating the stems from the leaves. Trim away any rough or tough part of the stems, usually on the bottom, finely chop the stems, and set aside. Chop the leaves, then swish them around in a basin or bowl and either spin dry in a salad spinner or let them drain very well in a colander.

Heat ½ cup of olive oil in a wide pot over medium heat. Sauté the leek, onion, fennel, carrot, and greens stems until soft, about 10 minutes. Stir in the garlic. Add the rice and stir to coat with the olive oil. Add greens in batches and stir to cook down, until all of the chard and spinach have been added.

Season with salt and pepper. Add 2 cups of vegetable stock. Cook over low heat, covered, until rice is very tender, about 45 minutes. Add more stock, if necessary, to keep the mixture moist and retain enough liquid for the rice to cook. The greens will let out their own liquid, too, so you have to use your judgment.

About 5 minutes before removing from heat, stir in all the fresh herbs and half the lemon juice. Stir in remaining olive oil and adjust seasoning with additional lemon juice, salt, and pepper to taste. Serve, if desired, with a small wedge or a little crumbled Greek feta or a few spoonfuls of plain Greek yogurt on top.

rice & beans, sort of!

Wild rice and quinoa are most certainly not native to Greece, but they have both found their place in the local kitchen. The combination of grains and beans, whether it be pasta, rice, wild rice, or quinoa, makes for a whole protein. This easy grains and beans dish is great for a weeknight dinner and is the kind of recipe that will hold up if you brown-bag it for lunch the next day!

MAKES 4 TO 6 SERVINGS

1 cup wild rice

2 pieces star anise

Sea salt to taste

1 cup quinoa

2 cups cooked and drained good-quality canned kidney beans

Grated zest of 1 orange

1 small chili pepper, seeded and finely chopped or minced

1 medium red onion, minced

2 garlic cloves, minced

FOR THE DRESSING

½ cup extra-virgin Greek olive oil

Juice of 1 orange

2 to 3 tablespoons balsamic vinegar

Dash hot sauce

Sea salt and freshly ground black pepper to taste

Place the wild rice and 1 star anise in a medium saucepan with enough water to cover by 3 inches. Bring to a boil, reduce heat to a simmer, add salt to taste, and cook until al dente but tender, about 40 to 50 minutes. Drain and remove the star anise.

While the wild rice is cooking, cook the quinoa, too. Place it in a separate medium pot with enough water to cover it by 3 inches. Season with salt and add the second star anise. Bring to a boil and simmer for about 5 minutes, or until tender. Drain well, remove the star anise, and fluff with a fork.

Combine the wild rice, quinoa, kidney beans, orange zest, minced chili pepper, onion, and garlic in a mixing bowl.

Whisk together the ingredients for the dressing. Add the dressing to the wild rice–quinoa–bean mixture, toss gently, and serve.

zucchini pilaf WITH AVOCADO & OLIVES

One recent end of summer on Ikaria taught me how to enjoy olives that had fallen to the ground. I had a friend over who was doing some woodwork for me, and he noticed that my garden was covered with olives that had fallen off the tree after a few exceptionally windy days. They were already quite mature, and he showed me how delicious they actually were, needing no curing at all, when he plucked one from the ground, rinsed it off, and popped it into his mouth, something I honestly wouldn't have thought of doing. I do love olives, and my favorites are the wrinkled olives that mature on the tree, much like the ones he showed me. There are a few well-known Greek varieties, including *throumbes* and *damaskinoelies*. They're sweet and pleasantly leathery, and they have a mild olive flavor with almost none of the palate-numbing saltiness of other cured olives.

It's that saltiness that sometimes turns people off to olives, but the fruit of the *Olea europaea* (European olive) is exceptionally nutritious. Olives are very rich in vitamin E and other antioxidants, which may help reduce the risk of health conditions like cancer, diabetes, stroke, and heart disease. They're a great source of vitamin A, copper, calcium, and iron, and the oleocanthal in olives (and olive oil) is linked to a reduced risk for Alzheimer's disease and dementia. Olives are, in other words, one of the world's most important superfoods!

MAKES 4 TO 6 SERVINGS

1½ cups regular or parboiled brown rice

¼ cup extra-virgin Greek olive oil

3 medium zucchinis, cut into 1-inch (2½-cm) cubes

Salt and freshly ground black pepper to taste

3 large garlic cloves, chopped

1 cup wrinkled black olives

Grated zest of 1 lemon

3 tablespoons fresh oregano or 1 teaspoon dried Greek oregano

1 large firm, ripe avocado, peeled and cut into ¾-inch cubes

Cook the rice in lightly salted water according to package directions.

While the rice is cooking, heat 2 tablespoons of olive oil in a large skillet over medium-high heat. Add the zucchini, season lightly with salt and pepper, and sear, in batches if necessary, until golden. Turn it gently in the pan to brown lightly on both sides. Stir in the garlic for about 45 seconds before removing the zucchini, being careful not to burn it. Remove the zucchini and garlic from the skillet and set aside.

Add the olives to the same skillet and warm over low heat, shaking back and forth, in whatever remaining olive oil is in the pan. Stir in the lemon zest.

When the rice is done, remove from heat and transfer to a large bowl. Gently toss the rice with the remaining 2 table-spoons of olive oil. Season to taste with salt and pepper and gently mix in the oregano, zucchini, olives, and avocado. Serve.

front
& center

PLANT-BASED MAIN COURSES

If there is one thing that sets apart the Ikarian table and wider Greek cooking traditions from other cuisines in the Mediterranean, it is the incredible wealth of plant-based main courses, so entrenched in how we eat that we really don't think about them much. Whether it's a traditional rice dish like the Longevity Greens Rice on page 181, a stuffed vegetable dish like Round Zucchini Stuffed with Rice, Corn & Herbs (page 208), a hearty bean or vegetable stew, like the Spicy Fava Beans Braised in Red Wine on page 139, or the Braised Cauliflower with Olives & Cinnamon on page 227, these recipes are almost always vegan save for the optional accompaniment of, say, a piece of healthy fermented cheese like feta. Plant-based foods have been front and center in the Greek kitchen forever.

There are a few reasons for that. One is religious: people still fast, and when one assiduously follows the Greek Orthodox calendar, that means going off most animal products (bloodless seafood is allowed) for about half the year. The other reason is socioeconomic: until fairly recently, most people simply couldn't afford to eat meat very regularly. In Ikaria, the most affluent families ate a little meat a few times a month or added bits of home-cured meats to vegetable or bean stews to enrich them and provide some protein to what used to be the big, sprawling families of old.

But the tradition of seeing plants as a protagonist is still very much part of how we think of food in Ikaria and more broadly in Greece. When I teach my classes, this, together with the profuse use of herbs, are the two most startling revelations for most guests. That plants can be satisfying and filling is a paradigm shift.

I've taken liberties in the recipes that follow by creating a mix of main courses that reflect contemporary trends and traditional dishes from the island. Fun, new dishes include a few vegetable steaks, which I have come to love as a cook for their dramatic presentation and ease of preparation, and Vegan Moussaka, which includes no processed vegan meats but rather a luscious "meaty" sauce made of black beans and chickpeas. A vegan bread pudding taps into the old-world custom of making good use of something as prosaic, and sacrosanct, as bread that's gone stale. Baked green beans with a wedge of feta was born after watching a viral melted feta and tomato video! But my traditionalist's soul couldn't omit a few stuffed vegetables, with the likes of rice and bulgur, and a few dishes in the *ladera* (olive oil) category—silky-smooth with generous amounts of Greek EVOO.

That plant-based ingredients with minimum use of cheese or dairy can stand alone as main courses is one of the greatest lessons of the Ikaria, and, indeed, the whole Greek table.

butternut squash steaks

WITH SAGE, MINT & PISTACHIOS

In the traditional diet of Ikaria, winter squashes are an important garden vegetable. Ironically, they are actually planted in the summer, as I plant mine, typically sometime in early July. By the time I leave the island in September, their big, heavy bodies sit like gnomes in the dirt waiting to be pulled up. You can also see them dangling from their vines down garden walls on walks around Raches, on the northern side of the island.

There are countless varieties of winter squash. Among my personal favorites is butternut, rich as it is in so many good things, especially vitamins A and C but also manganese, potassium, magnesium, vitamin E, vitamin B$_6$, folate, vitamin B$_1$, vitamin B$_2$, vitamin B$_3$, vitamin B$_5$, vitamin K, calcium, iron, phosphorus, zinc, copper, and selenium. That's a heady list of nutrients for a simple garden vegetable!

What I like most about butternuts, though, are their versatility, texture, and nutty flavor. Their smooth flesh does indeed feel a little like butter in the mouth, and they do taste a little, well, nutty, hence the name of this variety, which was born in Massachusetts in the 1940s. Butternuts are sturdy and will last unrefrigerated for weeks or even longer. On Ikaria, most people store them in the coolest part of the house or cellar or peel and freeze their flesh to use in traditional recipes like pies and casseroles. My Ikaria friends were surprised, to say the least, when I served them a couple of pan-seared butternut steaks. This simple recipe makes a great main course, served with a simple salad and/or a grain dish.

MAKES 2 SERVINGS

1 long-necked butternut squash, about 3 pounds (1.4 kilos)

3 tablespoons extra-virgin Greek olive oil

3 large garlic cloves, finely chopped

6 fresh sage leaves, chopped

1 small bunch mint, trimmed and chopped

4 tablespoons shelled salted or unsalted pistachios, coarsely chopped

1 tablespoon fresh strained lemon juice

1 tablespoon fresh strained orange juice

1 tablespoon balsamic vinegar

1 tablespoon pomegranate or grape molasses (*petimezi*)

Sea salt and freshly ground pepper to taste

Cut the tough stem off the squash. Cut the neck off, separating the longer part of the squash from the rounder base. Reserve the base for another use, for example, in soup. Cut the neck in half lengthwise. Peel and remove the seeds. Trim the rounded part of the slabs to form steaks and reserve the trimmings for another use, for soups, pilafs, pasta sauce, and so on.

Heat 1 tablespoon of olive oil in a large heavy skillet over medium heat. Cook squash steaks, turning every 3 to 4 minutes, until golden brown on both sides and fork-tender, about 15 minutes.

Push the steaks to one side of the skillet. Add the remaining olive oil, garlic, sage, mint, and nuts to skillet, tilt the pan toward you so the oil pools on one side, and use a large spoon to continually baste steaks. Cook, basting, for about 1 minute. Remove from heat and stir in lemon and orange juice, balsamic vinegar, and the pomegranate molasses or *petimezi*; season with salt and pepper.

Transfer squash steaks to plates and spoon sauce over them. Serve hot.

broccoli wedges & potatoes baked in paper

WITH OUZO, FETA & HERBS

In the Greek kitchen, star anise is mostly associated with distilled liqueurs like ouzo. I love its flavor and use it a lot in my cooking. It has a natural sweetness with a distinct licorice flavor that pairs so well with vegetables and enhances the ouzo that's already part of the marinade. Star anise has some pretty stellar health benefits, too. It is rich in antioxidants and vitamins A and C and is great for digestion.

MAKES 2 OR 4 SERVINGS

1 large broccoli head, tough part of stem trimmed

6 tablespoons extra-virgin Greek olive oil

3 tablespoons fresh lemon juice

2 tablespoons ouzo or other anise-flavored liqueur

3 teaspoons Dijon mustard

Salt and freshly ground black pepper to taste

2 Yukon Gold potatoes or 2 sweet potatoes, peeled, halved, and sliced into ⅛-inch rounds

4 small whole star anise pieces

1 medium red onion, chopped

1 medium firm, ripe tomato, cored and chopped

4 teaspoons small capers, drained

4 tablespoons chopped fresh flat-leaf parsley

4 tablespoons crumbled Greek feta

1 lemon, cut into 4 wedges

Using a sharp, large knife, cut the broccoli lengthwise into 4 wedges.

Whisk together 4 tablespoons of the olive oil, 1½ tablespoons lemon juice, ouzo, 2 teaspoons of mustard, salt, and pepper in a large wide bowl and marinate the broccoli, turning it to moisten on all sides, for 15 minutes. Marinate the potato slices in the remaining olive oil, lemon juice, and mustard, whisking the liquids together in a medium bowl and then turning the potato slices in it. Preheat the oven to 375°F (190°C).

Cut 4 pieces of parchment paper into about 7 or 8 inches square. Place a quarter of the potatoes in a single layer on the bottom of one piece of parchment, then add the marinated broccoli wedges over them. Add a star anise to each wedge. Repeat with remaining pieces of parchment, sprinkling equal amounts of the onions, tomatoes, capers, parsley, and feta over and around each wedge and drizzling each evenly with any remaining marinade. Fold the paper over the broccoli to make a secure parcel, turning the top edges in together to seal.

Lightly oil a baking dish large enough to hold all the parcels. Place the parcels seam-side up in the dish and sprinkle with a little water. Bake for about 40 minutes, or until the broccoli is tender. Serve on individual plates, each in its parcel, with a wedge of fresh lemon.

herby portobello steaks

WITH HEIRLOOM CARROT FAVA

The combination of mushrooms and legumes is popular in Greece, and it pops up nowadays on restaurant menus in Athens in what seems like a concerted effort among chefs to create plant-based main courses that are nutritious and delicious. Mushrooms are pretty amazing from a nutritional perspective: they contain comparable amounts of protein per 100 calories of most meats and are much richer in vitamins and minerals. They have always been an important food on Ikaria, arguably one of the island's longevity foods, providing everything from nourishment to natural exercise (foraging for them means walking for hours up and down the mountains) to a reason for inviting friends over for a tasty feast.

This simple recipe calls for what is probably the best large-cap mushroom for transforming into a meaty steak-like dish: the portobello. I like to marinate them in a mixture that includes sweet wine or sherry, the latter of which reminds me of local Ikarian wine, much of it bordering on sweet and quite strong. As for the fava—the puree of yellow split peas—you can make that a day ahead of time and serve it either warm or at room temperature.

MAKES 2 OR 4 SERVINGS

2 tablespoons balsamic vinegar

1 tablespoon soy or Worcestershire sauce

4 tablespoons sweet sherry or sweet red wine, such as port or Mavrodafni

½ teaspoon Dijon mustard

2 teaspoons sherry vinegar

2 teaspoons garlic paste or minced garlic

Sea salt and freshly ground black pepper to taste

1 teaspoon finely chopped fresh rosemary

1 teaspoon finely chopped fresh oregano

1 teaspoon finely chopped fresh thyme

4 tablespoons extra-virgin Greek olive oil, or more, as desired, plus 1 teaspoon for oiling the grill pan

4 large portobello mushrooms

½ recipe for Heirloom Carrot Fava (page 31)

Fresh thyme, rosemary, or oregano sprig for garnish

In a medium bowl, whisk together the balsamic vinegar, soy sauce, sweet wine, mustard, sherry vinegar, garlic paste, salt, pepper, herbs, and olive oil to make a smooth, emulsified liquid.

Remove the stems from the mushrooms and set aside for another use, for example, in soup, or discard.

Wipe the mushroom caps and undersides clean with a damp cloth. Drop the caps into the bowl with the marinade and turn a few times to coat. Set aside for 10 minutes.

Warm a ridged grill pan over medium-high heat and brush with 1 teaspoon of olive oil. Remove the portobello mushroom caps from marinade, letting any excess liquid drip off back into the bowl. Place the caps smooth-side down in the grill pan and gently press—being careful not to crack or break them—with a spatula. Grill on one side until the mushrooms are tender and lined with grill marks, then flip carefully to grill on the other side. Transfer to a platter, pour any remaining marinade into the grill pan, and heat for a minute or two over medium heat until it bubbles and thickens a little. Serve the mushrooms on the same plate as the fava, drizzle with the pan juices, and garnish with an herb sprig.

MAGIC MUSHROOMS

I wish I could make a scientific connection between the relatively low incidence of age-related cognitive disorders among older Ikarians and mushroom consumption. Mushrooms, mostly wild, have always been an important part of the local diet; there is an ever-growing body of scientific evidence linking regular mushroom consumption with a reduced threat of cognitive impairment. I can only sing the praises of mushrooms in many dishes inspired by the island's foodways and discuss parallel to that some of the wider body of evidence linking them to a healthier memory as we grow older.

A 2019 study in Singapore, reported in the *Journal of Alzheimer's Disease*, found evidence linking mushroom consumption to a reduction in mild cognitive impairment. A 2022 article in the journal *Brain Science* by Alzheimer's researcher Thalia Dimopoulos connects consumption of white button mushrooms to better spatial memory and reduced plaque formation in the brain. "One of the main theories for the causation of AD is the formation of amyloid-ß (Aß) plaques in the brain," explains Dimopoulos. A hundred grams of white button mushrooms contains 9.3 micrograms of selenium, an important antioxidant that may reduce ROS (reactive oxidative species), which basically means unstable oxygen atoms that can cause cell death and inflammation. We eat antioxidants so they can bind to oxygen and stabilize it. Mushrooms also contain potassium, phosphorus, and vitamins B_1, B_2, B_{12}, C, D, and E. "For centuries, mushrooms have been used as a source of homeopathy for oxidative stress-related illnesses," writes Dimopoulos. White button mushrooms, *Agaricus bisporus* (*A. bisporus*), the world's most common, "have been seen to be beneficial in metabolic syndrome, immune function, gastrointestinal health, and cancer; with

the strongest evidence for the improvement in Vitamin D status in humans," writes Dimopoulos.

The best rewards come from eating at least 2 portions per week, but closer to 3 portions per week reaped even more benefits. Dimopoulos explains: "Mushrooms are the most beneficial when you cook them until they're soft. The chitin (exterior wall) needs to break down to allow the trace minerals and protein to be digested and metabolized. Uncooked mushrooms aren't bad for you in any way, but you won't receive the bulk of their nutrients without cooking them. Also, the nutrients come almost exclusively from the caps and not the stems, so unless you want to feel fuller or just need extra weight in the dish, you can discard the stems or compost them."

All edible mushrooms are generally beneficial since funguses tend to hold onto a great deal of trace minerals and have a good amount of protein in them. Other, specific varieties that are known for their benefits in terms of cognition are turkey tail, lion's mane, maitake/hen-of-the-woods, shiitake, and oyster mushrooms, to name a few.

"The beauty of mushrooms is that you can cook them in any way you want and they'll absorb the flavors of the dish once that chitin breaks down," notes Dimopoulos. "From what I know, there's no wrong way to cook them since they are so versatile. Just speaking from my Alzheimer's experience, as much as we can avoid excess salt and saturated fats in general to keep the blood pressure down and prevent strokes, that's the best way we can cook, period [and, clearly, the Ikarian diet does this fabulously]. We have a saying in the Alzheimer's community: if you cook heart healthy, you automatically cook brain healthy. Same principles apply to preventing Alzheimer's and/or slowing it down if there's a diagnosis."

mushroom–red pepper souvlaki

WITH PISTACHIO PESTO

Mushroom souvlaki is a no-brainer for me, especially given both the popularity of skewered foods in Greece and the popularity and importance of mushrooms on Ikaria. Mushrooms offer immeasurable goodness! Studies show that consuming mushrooms as a regular part of your diet can help relieve hypertension, improve gut health, fight off cancer, and stave off diabetes. Mushrooms are one of the few plant-based sources of vitamin D, which is important in keeping COVID-19 and other illnesses at bay. They reduce inflammation and help lower cholesterol. They also have a meaty texture, so eating mushrooms is one way to help you reduce the consumption of red meat in your diet.

MAKES 4 SERVINGS

8 12-inch (30-cm) metal or wooden skewers

3 tablespoons extra-virgin Greek olive oil

3 tablespoons ouzo

2 tablespoons fresh strained lemon juice

3 large garlic cloves, minced

Greek sea salt to taste

1 teaspoon freshly ground black pepper

16 large cepes or white button mushrooms, halved, with their stems

4 red bell peppers, seeded and cut lengthwise into 8 wedges or strips

FOR THE PESTO

⅔ cup shelled unsalted pistachios

2 garlic cloves

2 bunches fresh mint, leaves only, coarsely chopped

¼ cup grated Parmigiano, Romano, or cashew-milk cheese of choice

3 tablespoons extra-virgin Greek olive oil

2 teaspoons grated fresh lemon zest

Freshly ground black pepper

Greek sea salt to taste

If using wooden as opposed to metal skewers, soak them in water for 30 minutes before using. Preheat the broiler. Place the oven rack 6 inches (15 cm) from the heat source. Line a baking sheet with parchment paper.

In a large bowl, whisk together the olive oil, ouzo, lemon juice, garlic, salt, and pepper.

Toss the mushroom halves and pepper strips in the marinade and leave for 5 minutes. Thread 4 mushroom halves and 4 red pepper strips onto 1 of each of the 8 skewers. Place on the prepared baking sheet and brush with any remaining marinade. Broil for 8 to 12 minutes, or until tender and lightly charred.

While the skewers are under the broiler, make the pesto: Pulverize the pistachios and garlic in a food processor. Add the mint and pulse on and off to mix. Add the cheese, olive oil, lemon zest, and pepper to taste. Pulse to combine. Season with salt to taste.

Remove the skewers from the oven and serve with the pesto.

tofu steaks

WITH MUSHROOMS, SHALLOTS & HERBS

Tofu is hardly a traditional ingredient in the longevity diet of Ikaria. But it is elsewhere, and it is available and widely embraced among plant-loving, health-conscious Greek cooks. I've embraced it, too, and have discovered that its versatility and mild flavor make it easy to add to the Mediterranean diet.

Look for organic tofu and stay away from any genetically modified soy products (tofu is soy-based). It has some surprising health benefits, especially for women over fifty. Tofu is rich in calcium and vitamin D, helps with bone health and osteoporosis, and has even been found to be helpful in easing the hot flashes associated with menopause.

MAKES 2 SERVINGS

1 12-ounce (340 g) block extra-firm organic tofu

6 tablespoons extra-virgin Greek olive oil

4 shallots, peeled, halved, and thinly sliced

1 large garlic clove, minced

Greek sea salt and freshly ground black pepper to taste

½ pound (225 g) cepes, button mushrooms, or shiitakes, trimmed

⅓ cup aromatic dry white wine, such as Greek chardonnay

3 tablespoons finely chopped fresh flat-leaf parsley

1 teaspoon dried tarragon

¼ cup potato starch or cornstarch

3 to 4 fresh tarragon or parsley sprigs for garnish, if desired

Cut the tofu in half across the middle to create two square blocks about ¾-inch thick each. The excess moisture in the tofu needs to be drained off, and there are a few ways to do this: you can either lightly salt and drain the tofu on a wire rack placed over a pan, with another pan set on top to press it down, or you can pat each piece dry with a paper towel and then microwave it for 45 seconds to dry it out.

Heat 2 tablespoons of olive oil in a large nonstick skillet over medium heat and sauté the shallots and garlic for 1 minute. Add the mushrooms. Season with salt and pepper, reduce heat to low, cover, and cook for about 8 minutes, until the mushrooms are softened but not mushy. Raise the heat on the mushrooms and add the wine. When it steams up and the alcohol cooks off, lower the heat and continue cooking for a few minutes, until the pan juices thicken. Remove from heat and stir in the parsley, tarragon, and a tablespoon of olive oil.

While the mushrooms are cooking, sear the tofu steaks: Season the prepared tofu with salt and pepper to taste, and sift the potato starch or cornstarch over each piece on both sides.

In a separate large nonstick skillet, heat 4 tablespoons olive oil over high heat and sear the tofu for about 1 to 2 minutes per side, or until crisp and golden brown.

Serve the tofu steaks on individual plates or a small platter and spoon the mushroom mixture on top and around them. Garnish with a few fresh tarragon or parsley sprigs if desired.

portobello mushrooms stuffed

WITH BRIAM

Briam is a classic Greek vegetable dish prepared with tomatoes, zucchini, eggplant, peppers, onions, and potatoes. It can be made as a stovetop stew or baked in the oven, and it's surprisingly versatile, making a great filling for just about everything from omelets to wraps to these stuffed portobello mushroom caps. The mushrooms themselves are so meaty and rich in flavor, one is probably enough for a satisfying main course.

Because they're so substantial, fleshy, and succulent, portobello mushrooms easily satisfy even the most tempting cravings for red meat. They're also the best mushroom for stuffing because their caps are large and deep. You can keep this recipe completely vegan by not adding any cheese or using the mature form of button and cremini mushrooms. All of these mushrooms are in fact the same species at different stages of maturity. Portobellos are rich in flavor, and their texture is meatier and less spongy than button mushrooms because as they grow, they lose moisture and so become denser. Because of their large size, they can be stuffed, baked, broiled, and grilled. Portobello mushrooms average around 6 inches across and have a dark brown color and firm texture.

MAKES 4 OR 8 SERVINGS

8 large portobello
mushrooms, with caps about
5 to 6 inches (12 to 15 cm)
in diameter

⅓ cup extra-virgin
Greek olive oil

1 large red onion, diced

1 medium Yukon Gold
or other waxy potato,
peeled and cut into ¼-inch
(1-cm) dice

1 medium eggplant, cut into
½-inch (1½-cm) dice

1 large green or red bell
pepper, seeded and finely
chopped

1 medium zucchini, cut into
¼-inch (1-cm) dice

3 garlic cloves, minced

½ cup dry white wine

⅔ cup crushed canned
tomatoes, drained

1 tablespoon balsamic vinegar

Salt and freshly ground
black pepper to taste

2 teaspoons
dried Greek oregano,
or more to taste

⅔ cup grated
Greek Kefalotyri cheese,
Parmigiano, Romano,
or grated vegan cashew-milk
cheese

If the mushrooms come with stems, remove, trim, and chop them. Set the caps aside on a lightly oiled baking dish large enough to hold them in one layer. Preheat the oven to 350°F (175°C).

Heat the olive oil in a large skillet and cook the onion over medium heat, stirring occasionally, until very soft, about 10 minutes. Add the potato, eggplant, bell pepper, and mushroom stems, if using, stir to coat the oil. Cover and steam in the oil for about 5 minutes until everything is softened and translucent. Stir in the zucchini and cook for about two minutes, Stir in the garlic.

Add the wine and as soon as it cooks off, in about five minutes, add the tomatoes and balsamic vinegar. Raise heat and simmer, uncovered, for about 7 minutes until the juices have all cooked off. Season to taste with salt and pepper, remove from heat, and gently stir in the oregano.

Let the mixture cool. Then fill each of the portobello caps with a mound of the briam mixture. Sprinkle the stuffed mushrooms with half the grated cheese. Cover the baking pan loosely with parchment and aluminum foil and bake the mushrooms for about 20 minutes, until soft. Remove the mushrooms from the oven, uncover, and sprinkle them with the remaining cheese. Put them back in the oven, under the broiler this time, until the cheese and vegetables start to char.

Remove and serve.

honeynut squash stuffed

WITH GARLIC, HERBS & MUSHROOMS

Honeynut squash is a relatively new squash variety from Upstate New York, the result of a collaboration between a Cornell professor and Chef Dan Barber. It looks like a smaller version of a butternut squash, but its skin is edible and much thinner, and it changes from green to orange as the squash ripens. It's delicious roasted or stuffed and has a sweet, nutty flavor. You can enjoy this stuffed honeynut recipe skin and all!

MAKES 4 TO 6 SERVINGS

2 honeynut squashes, about 8 to 10 inches (20 to 25 cm) long, or 2 small butternut squashes

3 tablespoons dry red wine

4 tablespoons extra-virgin Greek olive oil

3 garlic cloves, minced

Salt and freshly ground black pepper

3 fresh rosemary sprigs

1 tablespoon juniper berries

FOR THE STUFFING

3 tablespoons extra-virgin Greek olive oil

4 scallions, trimmed and chopped

1 large red or yellow onion, chopped

2 large garlic cloves, minced

Greek sea salt and freshly ground black pepper to taste

1 pound (450 g) mushrooms, wiped clean, trimmed, and chopped

2 tablespoons chopped fresh oregano

1 tablespoon chopped fresh thyme

4 tablespoons chopped fresh flat-leaf parsley

2 tablespoons coarsely chopped toasted hazelnuts

1 cup crumbled Greek feta or coarsely grated mild yellow cheese such as Kefalograviera, Kefalotyri, gruyere, or asiago, divided (optional)

Preheat the oven to 400°F (200°C). Cut the squashes in half lengthwise. Using a spoon, scoop out and discard the seeds. Line a baking sheet with parchment paper.

Whisk together the red wine, olive oil, garlic, salt, and pepper. Place the squash halves cut-side up on the lined baking sheet and brush with the marinade. Turn them cut-side down and brush the skins with any remaining marinade. Nestle the rosemary sprigs and juniper berries between the squash halves. Bake for about 20 to 25 minutes, or until the squash flesh is soft. (If you're using butternuts, which have a thicker skin, you may need to roast them for a few minutes longer.) Remove and cool. Lower the oven temperature to 375°F (190°C). Discard the rosemary and juniper from the sheet pan.

While the squash is roasting, prepare the mushroom filling: In a medium skillet, heat the 3 tablespoons of olive oil over medium-high heat and sauté the onion and scallions until translucent, about 5 to 6 minutes, stirring. Add the garlic and swirl around for about a minute. Add the mushrooms and sauté until they no longer exude liquid and the skillet is relatively dry. Season with salt and pepper and remove from heat. Let the mixture cool slightly.

Carefully scoop out the flesh from the squash and transfer it to a mixing bowl. Mash it slightly in the bowl with a fork. Add the mushroom mixture to the bowl. Add the herbs and half the cheese, if using.

Fill the cavities of the squash with the mushroom mixture and sprinkle with $\frac{1}{2}$ tablespoon each of the chopped toasted hazelnuts and the remaining cheese, if using, and set back onto the sheet pan. Bake for about 10 minutes, or until the filling starts to brown lightly and the cheese, if using, starts to melt. If you're using a larger squash, cut each half into pieces to ensure that each serving includes some of the squash and the filling. Serve hot.

eggplant boats stuffed WITH BULGUR, TOMATOES & BASIL

Eggplant has a special place in the cooking of the Eastern Aegean and Eastern Mediterranean. It is said that there are a thousand recipes for this popular summer vegetable. This one is inspired by older island versions of stuffed vegetables when bulgur was more common than rice. Indeed, rice, not native to Greece, was once a luxury food reserved for holiday and wedding dishes and to feed sick people. Although rice has been cultivated in Greece since the middle of the twentieth century, recipes for vegetables (and meats) stuffed with bulgur still abound in the Aegean.

MAKES 4 OR 8 SERVINGS

½ cup bulgur wheat

1 cup boiling water

4 medium eggplants, about 5 to 6 inches long

4 tablespoons extra-virgin Greek olive oil

Sea salt and freshly ground black pepper

1 medium red onion, chopped finely

3 garlic cloves, minced

1 teaspoon dried Greek oregano

1 pinch cayenne pepper

1 pinch smoked paprika

1 pound (450 g) fresh plum tomatoes (about 8), cored, seeded, and chopped

2 teaspoons sherry vinegar

1 bunch fresh basil, stems trimmed and leaves roughly chopped

2 tablespoons pine nuts, lightly toasted

Preheat the oven to 375°F (190°C). Line a baking sheet with parchment paper.

Place the bulgur in a medium bowl and pour the water over it. Let the bulgur soak until it expands, softens, and absorbs all the liquid, about 30 minutes. You can also prepare the bulgur ahead of time: Place it in a mixing bowl with 1 cup of room temperature water and leave it to soak, covered with a kitchen towel, for about 1½ to 2 hours, until it absorbs all the water and is tender but firm. Set it aside until ready to use.

In the meantime, halve the eggplants lengthwise, and score the flesh of each half in a 1-inch diamond pattern, about ½-inch deep. Brush the scored sides of eggplant with 2 tablespoons of oil and season with salt and pepper. Lay the eggplant halves, cut-side down, on the baking sheet, and roast until the flesh is tender and cooked, about 40 to 45 minutes. Remove from the oven and set aside to cool.

Heat the remaining 2 tablespoons oil in a 12-inch skillet over medium heat until shimmering. Add the onion and garlic and cook until softened, about 8 minutes. Season with spices and salt and pepper. Turn off the heat, stir in swollen bulgur, tomatoes, basil, and vinegar, and let sit about 1 minute. Season with salt and pepper to taste.

Return the eggplant halves cut-side up to the sheet. Using a teaspoon, carefully remove the eggplant flesh, leaving each of the eggplant shells intact and about ⅛-inch thick around the perimeter, thick enough to hold the filling.

Chop the eggplant flesh and add it to the bulgur mixture. Mix well and adjust the seasoning.

Mound the filling into the eggplant shells, sprinkle with pine nuts, and bake for 20 minutes. Serve.

round zucchini stuffed

WITH RICE, CORN & HERBS

This is the ultimate late-summer treat, when corn, zucchini, and tomatoes are all ripe and bursting with flavor. Zucchini, summer's low-calorie, fiber-rich prize, rich in vitamins B_6, C, and A, potassium, and folate, is very popular in Ikaria. There are a few traditional ways to prepare it, some a little healthier than others. Cut into finger-thick sticks and breaded, zucchini is a beloved fry, especially on the meze menus of local tavernas. It is made into patties (see page 45) that are either baked or pan-fried in olive oil, and it's a favorite protagonist in many savory pies. But some of the best recipes, both traditional and inspired by the island, at least to this cook, call for stuffing it.

MAKES 4 OR 8 SERVINGS

8 round zucchinis
or 4 regular zucchinis,
about 6 inches long

Greek sea salt and freshly
ground black pepper to taste

¼ cup extra-virgin
Greek olive oil, or more,
as desired

3 medium red or yellow
onions, finely chopped

2 large shallots,
finely chopped

1 fennel bulb, trimmed and
finely chopped

4 large garlic cloves, minced

⅔ cup long-grain parboiled
brown rice or white rice

1⅓ cups vegetable broth
or stock, plus ½ cup

1 cup fresh or frozen and
defrosted corn kernels

Finely grated zest of 1 lemon

½ cup finely
chopped fresh parsley

½ cup finely
chopped fresh mint

½ cup finely
chopped fresh basil

½ cup finely
chopped fresh dill

4 fresh plum tomatoes,
seeded and diced

Preheat oven to 350°F (175°C).

Slice the tops off the zucchini about ½ inch (a little more than a centimeter) from the stem. Reserve the tops. Using a teaspoon or melon baller, scoop out the pulp, making sure to leave about a ¼ inch of thickness inside each of the hollowed-out zucchinis so they retain their shape. Chop the pulp and set it aside until you're ready to use it.

Place the hollowed-out zucchini in a baking dish. Season the insides lightly with salt and pepper and turn them open-side down in the dish. Let them stand until ready to fill.

In a large deep frying pan over medium heat, warm 2 tablespoons of olive oil and cook the onions, shallot, and fennel until translucent, about 8 minutes. Stir in the garlic. Add the rice and toss to coat it in the oil. Add 1⅓ cups of vegetable broth or stock, reduce heat to low, and cook the rice, covered, for about 10 to 12 minutes, or until it has absorbed most of the liquid and is softened but al dente.

Next, add the reserved chopped zucchini pulp to the skillet and cook for about 5 minutes to draw out some of its moisture. Add the corn kernels and toss to combine. Remove from heat and stir in the lemon zest, herbs, and tomatoes. Season to taste with salt and pepper.

Spoon the filling into the round zucchini shells, top with the zucchini caps, and drizzle with remaining tablespoon of olive oil (or more, as desired). If there is leftover filling, you can spread it around the zucchini or bake it separately with additional water or broth in another baking dish. Pour the remaining ½ cup of broth or stock into the baking dish. Cover with parchment and aluminum foil, or with the lid, if there is one, and bake for about 45 minutes to 1 hour, or until the zucchini is fork-tender.

evangelia's lemony stove-top stuffed zucchini

When we meet for our welcome dinner during my Ikaria cooking weeks, I almost invariably take people to Nas, a small village on the northwestern tip of the island and the site of a fifth-century BCE temple to the goddess Artemis. Nas is also home to one of my favorite tavernas, Naiades, which means "mermaid," a name that references its proximity to the water and the fact that it's owned and operated by three generations of women: Evangelia, her two daughters, and now her granddaughter. It's been a farm-to-table little place long before that was ever a term in anyone's vocabulary. Almost everything comes from the family garden, including the wine. Evangelia is a traditional cook, and her food is simple and honest. This recipe, for an Ikarian classic, is one of my favorites. It never fails to surprise my guests, as a great example of satisfying, flavorful plant-based fare that is at the heart of so much food here.

Evangelia makes the dish with avgolemono, the traditional egg-lemon liaison that is a significant and versatile technique in Greek cooking. But long before there was ever a thought of creating egg substitutes, Greek cooks had to contend with the quandary of what to make in times of fasting, and so a simple preparation called *alevrolemono*—flour and lemon—was born. That's what's used to create the creamy, thick lemony sauce that graces this dish. There are instructions for the classic rendition following this recipe.

MAKES 4 SERVINGS

6 zucchinis, about 7 inches (17.5 cm) long

Sea salt

½ cup extra-virgin Greek olive oil, plus 2 tablespoons for the sauce

4 large onions, finely chopped

2 scallions or spring onions, trimmed and finely chopped

3 garlic cloves, minced

½ teaspoon fennel seeds, ground in a mortar and pestle or a spice grinder, or more to taste

⅔ cup medium-grain rice, such as sushi rice or Greek "stuffing" rice, which you can find in Greek shops and online

⅓ cup dry white wine

3 cups vegetable stock or water for the rice

Sea salt and freshly ground black pepper to taste

Grated zest of 1 lemon

1 cup finely chopped fresh dill, feathery leaves only

½ cup chopped fresh mint leaves

½ cup chopped fresh flat-leaf parsley

1 to 2 Yukon Gold potatoes, as needed

Fresh strained juice of 2 lemons

1 tablespoon all-purpose flour

2 large eggs (optional) (see Note)

Trim the ends off the zucchinis to create a flat surface on both ends so you can stand them upright in a large pot. Cut the zucchinis in half across the width to create 2 cylinders, each about 4 inches long. Hollow out each half carefully, using a teaspoon. I find the easiest way to do this is to cup each cylinder, one at a time in one hand and, using a teaspoon and gentle, circular motions, work my way through the zucchini cylinder to remove its pulp. Reserve the pulp.

Lightly salt the insides of each zucchini cylinder and place it cut-side down on a flat plate to drain a little. Finely chop the reserved pulp.

Warm 3 tablespoons of olive oil in a large deep frying pan over medium heat and cook the onion and scallion until wilted and translucent, about 7 to 8 minutes. Stir in the garlic and swirl it around for about 30 seconds to soften it. Add the fennel seeds and stir for a few seconds, then add the rice, reduce the heat to medium-low, and stir to toss in the oil. Pour in the wine, raise the heat to medium, and as soon as it steams up and the alcohol cooks off, add 1 cup of the stock or water. Season lightly with salt and pepper.

Cover and cook the rice mixture until the rice absorbs the liquid and is al dente, about 10 minutes. Stir the chopped zucchini pulp into the rice mixture and cook until it exudes most of its water and wilts, another 5 to 6 minutes. The rice should be tender but firm, and the contents of the frying pan juicy but not runny. Stir in the grated lemon zest and herbs. Taste and adjust the seasoning with additional salt and pepper. Set the rice filling aside to cool a little. Gently stir in another 2 tablespoons of olive oil to the rice mixture.

In a wide pot large enough to hold the zucchini upright in one layer and deep enough to keep each upright cylinder covered, drizzle in the remaining olive oil. Take 1 cylinder at a time and, using a teaspoon or tablespoon, fill it with the rice mixture, leaving about ⅛-inch space at the top. Place the cylinders upright in the pot.

Peel one of the potatoes and cut it into large 1-inch (2½-cm) cubes. Tuck the potato cubes between the zucchini cylinders to keep them snug and steady. Cut the second potato if more is needed to fill the gaps. Add enough water or stock to the pot to come about one-third of the way up the height of the cylinders. Cover the pot and bring it to a simmer over medium-high heat. Reduce heat to low and simmer the stuffed zucchini until the vegetables are fork-tender but not mushy, and the rice soft, about 35 minutes. The zucchini will release its liquid into the pot, and there should be plenty by the time the dish is ready.

About 7 minutes before removing from heat, whisk the lemon juice and flour together in a medium bowl and add a ladleful of the hot pan juices to the mixture in a slow, steady stream, whisking all the while to beat out any clumps. Pour this into the pan, tilting it so it is evenly distributed, and continue simmering over low heat until the juices are thick and creamy.

NOTE: If you opt to make a traditional avgolemono: Whisk the eggs in a medium metal bowl with vigor, until they are frothy and voluminous, for about 5 to 6 minutes. Slowly drizzle in the lemon juice, continuing to whisk fast. The color and consistency will change. The eggs will thicken and look like a pale yellow cream. Next, carefully extract a ladleful or cupful of hot pan juices from the zucchini and very slowly drizzle it into the creamy egg mixture. It should take you at least 2 minutes to empty that first cup or ladleful of pan juices while you whisk very quickly. Continue to do this, adding the hot pan juices very slowly to the eggs to temper them. Try to extract all or as much of the pan juices as possible, tilting the pan carefully as needed, and drizzle and whisk into the egg mixture. When most of the pan juices are mixed with the eggs, pour the whole mixture back into the pot and tilt it around to swirl all the juices together. Serve immediately. Do not cover the pot at this point because the eggs will curdle or cake up like an omelet! You can stabilize the egg-lemon mixture a little more if you also whisk in a scant teaspoon of cornstarch to the eggs before adding the lemon juice at the start of the process.

layered summer vegetables baked

WITH FETA CREAM

This recipe is an adaptation of a traditional Cretan dish called *mirabeliotika*, basically, baked, layered summer vegetables. I have tweaked it over the years and adapted it to whatever is growing in my summer garden. The original dish calls for pan-frying each vegetable separately before layering them all together and baking them, a technique cooks shun nowadays in favor of less time-consuming and fattening methods of softening the vegetables to be layered. Baking them off does the trick just as well and with good flavor. It's really important to make this dish in season when everything is at its peak.

MAKES 8 SERVINGS

3 pounds (1.4 kilos) firm, ripe tomatoes

½ cup extra-virgin Greek olive oil

4 garlic cloves, minced

Salt and freshly ground black pepper

1 tablespoon dried Greek oregano

1 to 2 tablespoons *petimezi* to taste (optional)

2 teaspoons balsamic vinegar

FOR THE VEGETABLES

1½ pounds (680 g) Yukon Gold or other waxy potatoes (about 5 to 6) peeled and sliced into ovals about ⅛-inch thick

Extra-virgin Greek olive oil as needed

Sea salt and freshly ground black pepper to taste

3 medium zucchinis, trimmed and cut into ¼-inch-thick slices

3 medium eggplants, trimmed and cut into ¼-inch-long slices

1½ cups crumbled Greek feta

½ to 1 cup ricotta, Greek *anthotyro*, or Greek yogurt

Preheat the oven to 350°F (175°C). Line 2 to 3 baking sheets with parchment paper.

Make the sauce: Hold the tomatoes from the stem end and grate them along the coarse side of a stand grater. You can do this with the grating attachment of a food processor as well, but doing it manually results in a better texture. Set tomatoes aside.

Heat the olive oil in a wide pot over medium-low heat and add the garlic. Cook it for a minute or so, until softened. Don't let it brown. Add the grated tomatoes, season with salt and pepper, and simmer uncovered until thick, about 45 minutes. Stir in the oregano, *petimezi*, and balsamic vinegar right before removing from heat.

While the sauce is simmering, prepare the vegetables: Toss the potato slices in a large mixing bowl with enough olive oil to moisten them, season them lightly with salt and pepper, then place them in neat, snug rows, overlapping slightly to make room, on the lined baking sheets. Bake until they can be pierced with a fork but are still a bit firm and al dente, about 12 to 15 minutes. Remove and transfer to a platter.

Repeat the same procedure with the zucchini and eggplant slices, baking until softened but firm. Remove from the oven and set aside.

Lightly oil a 12 × 18-inch ovenproof glass baking dish. Place the feta and ½ cup of the ricotta, *anthotyro*, or the Greek yogurt in the bowl of a food processor and process on medium-high speed until smooth. Add more of the ricotta/*anthotyro* or yogurt if the mixture is too dense. It should be creamy and smooth.

Spread the potato slices in one slightly overlapping layer on the bottom of the baking dish. Spoon about a third of the sauce over them and dot with the cheese mixture. Next, add the eggplant, a little more sauce and cheese, and then the zucchini, followed by the remaining sauce and cheese mixture, spreading it evenly over the top. Bake uncovered for about 50 minutes, or until set and golden. Remove, cool slightly, and serve. You can serve this at room temperature, too.

jammy braised chestnuts & onions

I've always loved the idea of using hearty chestnuts in savory dishes. Chestnuts are a good source of many vitamins and minerals, such as copper, manganese, vitamin B$_6$, vitamin C, thiamine, folate, riboflavin, and potassium. They are also a good source of fiber, with 15 percent of the daily recommended amount in ten roasted chestnuts. Chestnuts contain a variety of antioxidants, such as vitamin C, gallic acid, ellagic acid, tannins, and more. These antioxidants help defend your cells against free radical damage, which is linked to numerous chronic diseases. Chestnuts are high in fiber, which may help you lose weight by slowing down the digestion of food and curbing your appetite. They also contain fewer calories than other varieties of nuts due to their low fat content.

MAKES 4 TO 6 SERVINGS

3 tablespoons extra-virgin Greek olive oil

4 medium red onions, peeled, halved, and thickly sliced

4 garlic cloves, chopped

2 packets sous vide vacuum-packed chestnuts, blanched as per package directions, and separated

1½ cups chopped canned plum tomatoes

Sea salt and freshly ground black pepper to taste

⅔ cup dry white wine

2 tablespoons *petimezi*

2 tablespoons red wine or balsamic vinegar to taste

1 cinnamon stick

1 dried bay leaf

1 tablespoon tomato paste

1 pinch dried Greek oregano

3 to 4 sprigs dried thyme sprigs

Heat the olive oil in a deep, wide skillet over low-medium heat and cook the onions, stirring occasionally, until deeply caramelized, about 30 minutes.

Stir the garlic into the caramelized onions and then add the chestnuts, mixing them in gently.

Add the tomatoes and stir around with a wooden spoon. Season with salt and pepper. Add the wine, *petimezi*, balsamic vinegar, cinnamon stick, and bay leaf. Cook all together for about 40 minutes, or until thick and jammy. Stir in the tomato paste, cook for a few more minutes to thicken even more, and season with the oregano and thyme. Adjust seasoning with salt and pepper and serve.

vegan bread pudding

WITH GREENS & PEPPERS

Americans have an inglorious habit of throwing away about a third of everything we cook, disdaining leftovers! To me, the art of transforming leftovers into a new dish the next day is part of the joy of cooking. Stale, leftover bread has always played a role in the country cooking of the entire Mediterranean. In Greece, there are plenty of old regional recipes for making good use of stale bread, from our litany of dips like *skordalia* (garlic, bread, broth, and olive oil) to old village recipes that called for searing stale, cubed bread in olive oil and marrying those ingredients with everything from broths to tomato paste and herbs. It's a life lesson to make use of everything, reducing food waste and re-embracing a respect for one of the world's most sacred foods—bread! This recipe can easily double as a Thanksgiving stuffing that vegans, vegetarians, and carnivores alike will love.

MAKES 6 SERVINGS

10 cups trimmed bread cubes, 1 inch (2½ cm) square, from stale bread, preferably sourdough and/or whole grain

6 tablespoons extra-virgin Greek olive oil

Sea salt to taste

2 large leeks

1 large fennel bulb

5 garlic cloves, finely chopped

3 roasted red peppers in brine, drained and coarsely chopped

1 cup chopped fresh mint

1 teaspoon finely chopped fresh rosemary

2 teaspoons finely chopped fresh thyme

1 teaspoon dried Greek oregano

Freshly ground black pepper to taste

⅓ cup Corinthian currants

6 dried Greek figs, coarsely chopped

1 cup kalamata olives or other Greek olives, pitted and coarsely chopped

½ cup coarsely ground walnuts

1 cup Parmigiano-Reggiano or cashew-milk parmesan (optional)

3 cups vegetable broth or stock, or more, as needed

Preheat the broiler. Cut the bread into 1-inch ($2\frac{1}{2}$ cm) cubes, place on a baking sheet, drizzle with 3 tablespoons of olive oil, then sprinkle with and toss in the sea salt. Toast under the broiler, 8 inches (20 cm) from the heat source. Turn the bread cubes a few times while broiling to brown on all sides. The bread should be golden brown but not charred. Remove and set aside to cool.

Trim the roots and tough green tops off the leeks and halve the leeks lengthwise. Cut into thin slices. Place in a basin or in the bowl of a salad spinner with ample water and swish the leeks around to dislodge any sand or dirt. Remove the leeks by hand to a colander or the strainer and repeat a few times until the water comes clean. Drain the leeks very well in the colander or place them in the strainer part of the salad spinner and spin to dry.

Trim and coarsely chop the fennel, going up the stems as well but discarding any tough or woody parts. If there are feathery leaves on the fennel stalks, chop them, too.

Heat the olive oil in a deep, wide skillet over medium heat and sauté the leeks and fennel together until soft and translucent. Add the chopped garlic and stir it around for $\frac{1}{2}$ minute or so to soften. Add the roasted red peppers to the mixture and stir.

Switch from broiler to oven mode and preheat to 375°F (190°C).

Trim and chop the herbs. Combine the toasted bread cubes, onion-fennel-red pepper mixture, and herbs in a mixing bowl. Add the figs, currants, olives, ground walnuts, pepper, and all but 3 tablespoons of the Parmigiano-Reggiano and fold everything in together. If you opt to use vegan cheese, stir it in at this point as well.

Oil a 9 × 9-inch ($22\frac{1}{2}$ × 22-cm) ovenproof glass or ceramic baking dish. Add 2 cups of vegetable broth, or more if necessary, for the mixture to be moist but not soupy. Sprinkle with the remaining cheese. Bake for 30 minutes until puffy, slightly charred, and golden-brown.

pumpkin onion skillet pie in two versions

For this dish think tarte Tatin, but a more primitive, Aegean island rendition! I love this old dish, which is made in various versions, with and without cheese, on a few different islands in the Eastern Aegean. Together with a gaggle of local cooks, I made a Naxos version of it for season three of *My Greek Table*, and I was surprised to discover it was a traditional recipe from the island because I had always associated a dish like this with a deliciously similar and richer version made on Samos, which calls for crumbled feta or any soft goat's milk cheese. Winter squashes are important in the local diet of Ikaria and most Aegean islands. People grow them in their gardens and use them as the centerpiece in stews, savory phyllo pies, and dishes like this, layered without pastry and slowly cooked until all the delicious natural sugars in both the onions and winter squash caramelize to golden deliciousness.

MAKES 2 10- OR 12-INCH SKILLET PIES, OR 8 TO 12 MAIN SERVINGS

1 pumpkin or butternut squash, about 3 pounds (1.4 kilos)

3 large red onions, halved and cut into thin slices

Salt and freshly ground black pepper to taste

½ to ⅔ cup all-purpose flour, or as needed

4 to 8 tablespoons extra-virgin Greek olive oil, or as needed

1 cup crumbled Greek feta, divided (optional)

Peel and deseed the pumpkin or butternut squash. Cut the flesh into sticks or crescents about ¼-inch thick and 3 inches long. They won't be exact or consistent in size, but don't worry about that. They just need to be more or less all about the same size and thickness.

Place the squash pieces in a large bowl, mix in the onions, and season with salt and pepper. Sprinkle 3 tablespoons of flour over the mixture and turn with your hands to combine. Keep adding more flour in tablespoon increments until the mixture just starts to get a little sticky.

Warm 2 tablespoons of olive oil in a 10- or 12-inch non-stick frying pan over medium heat.

If you're planning to add cheese, then add ¼ of the mixture to the frying pan, sprinkle half the cheese evenly over the surface, and place another ¼ of the squash and onion mixture on top, spreading it evenly. With the back of a large spoon or spatula, flatten and pat the mixture down in the pan. Cover and cook for about 15 minutes, or until the bottom is lightly charred and crispy. Remove from heat, uncover, and place a large plate, big enough to cover the entire circumference of the frying pan with room to spare, over the pan. Using oven mitts, carefully flip the frying pan so that the crusty side is on top. Add a little more olive oil to the pan, turn the heat back on to low, and slide the now dense and solid pumpkin-onion mass back into the frying pan, with the browned side on top. Raise the heat to medium and continue to cook, covered, for about 12 to 15 minutes, or until the other side is also browned and crispy. Remove to a platter and keep covered to keep warm. Repeat the process with the remaining 2 batches of pumpkin–onion mixture and cheese.

If you opt to do this without cheese, then add half the mixture to the frying pan, patting it down to flatten, and cook in exactly the same way, until crispy on the bottom, then flip it to cook on the other side.

Cut the crispy skillet pies into 4 or 6 wedges each and serve hot or at room temperature, together with a simple green salad.

baked green beans

WITH CREAMY FETA

There is something, well, lusciously seductive about baked melting feta swirled into baked vegetables. This recipe plays off a very traditional green bean ragout that is a classic Ikarian and wider Greek recipe called *fasolakia yiahni*. Without the accompaniment of feta, it's a Lenten classic and totally vegan, but it is often served alongside a wedge of Greece's national cheese. In this recipe, cheese and beans are combined in one casserole, and the result is a creamy, satisfying combination that's hard not to love!

MAKES 6 SERVINGS

1½ pounds (680 g) fresh or frozen green beans, trimmed

4 tablespoons extra-virgin Greek olive oil

1 large red onion, coarsely chopped

Greek sea salt to taste

4 garlic cloves, minced

2 cups cherry or teardrop tomatoes, halved

2 tablespoons balsamic vinegar

1 tablespoon *petimezi* (optional)

1 heaping teaspoon dried Greek oregano

Finely grated zest of 1 lemon

1 2½-inch square of Greek feta about ¾-inch thick

Preheat the oven to 350°F (175°C).

Bring a large pot of salted water to a boil and blanch the green beans for 1 minute. Drain and set aside. Alternatively, you can steam the beans to soften them.

Heat 2 tablespoons of olive oil in a large frying pan over medium heat and cook the onions with a little salt until wilted and lightly browned, about 15 minutes.

Add the garlic to the onions and stir for about ½ a minute to soften the garlic. Add the halved tomatoes and stir them gently into the onion–garlic mixture. In about 7 minutes, as the tomatoes start to exude their juices and bubble a little in the pan, add the balsamic vinegar and *petimezi* and gently stir to combine.

Place the drained green beans and tomato–onion–garlic mixture in a baking dish. Toss with the remaining 2 table-spoons of olive oil. Mix in the oregano and lemon zest. Place the feta in the middle of the casserole and bake for 20 to 25 minutes, or until the feta is very soft.

Remove, and mix all together so the feta melts and is distributed evenly throughout the beans. Serve.

eggplant stewed WITH *TRAHANA*

I couldn't not include at least one recipe for *trahana* in a book inspired by Ikaria. *Trahana* is one of the most ancient grain products in the world, versions of which are still made all over the Eastern Mediterranean and Middle East. There are many regional variations of this pebbly, tangy grain preparation, which began as a way to preserve milk. In the loosest terms, it is made by cooking together bulgur or cracked wheat with milk, usually goat's milk, which adds depth of flavor and aromatic complexity to the mix. Then, once it is simmered to a density of overcooked oatmeal, it's broken into clumps, dried in the sun, then passed through a sieve to crumble into pebbles, which are dried further under the hot Greek summer sun. People still make it at home on Ikaria and across Greece, and it's often made in monasteries and sold—one of many artisanal foods—the sales of which help support these often isolated refuges. You can find *trahana* online and in Greek shops, too; different islands produce different shapes, from cups to little nuggets to pebbles. Although there are many different types, the basic delineation is into sweet and sour, sweet being made with whole milk and mild in flavor; sour being made with goat's milk, buttermilk, or tart Greek yogurt.

Trahana can be cooked alone and made into a filling porridge—the breakfast meal of old island farmers—or added to a whole host of stews and casseroles like this one. You can use coarse bulgur in its place, but you won't get that same delicious tart flavor!

MAKES 4 TO 6 SERVINGS

½ cup extra-virgin Greek olive oil

1 large red onion, coarsely chopped

3 garlic cloves, coarsely chopped

3 Italian or Sicilian eggplants, trimmed and cut into 1½-inch (3¾-cm) chunks or cubes, about 8 cups total

4 large ripe tomatoes, grated or finely chopped, or 3 cups chopped canned tomatoes and their juices

½ cup dry white wine

⅔ cup sour *trahana*

1 cup vegetable stock or water

Salt and freshly ground black pepper to taste

2 tablespoons chopped fresh oregano

3 tablespoons chopped fresh thyme

2 tablespoons chopped fresh parsley

2 tablespoons chopped fresh mint

Heat the olive oil in a wide pot over medium heat. Add the onions and cook, stirring, until soft, about 10 minutes. Stir in the garlic. Add the eggplant pieces and stir gently for 2 minutes, until coated in the oil, glistening, and starting to soften.

Add the tomatoes, bring to a simmer, and add the wine. Cook for about 5 to 7 minutes, until the alcohol has evaporated.

Stir in the *trahana*, toss it to combine, and add the vegetable stock or water to come to about 1 inch below the contents of the pot. Season with salt and pepper to taste. Lower the heat, partially cover the pot, and cook the eggplant and *trahana* until both are tender, about 20 minutes. Adjust the liquid content as needed with additional vegetable stock or water—the mixture should be dense and almost creamy, not soupy.

Stir in the herbs and remaining olive oil and serve.

VARIATION

This recipe can also be made with cauliflower instead of eggplant. Indeed, cauliflower stewed with *trahana* is one of the ultimate Aegean comfort food recipes! Replace the eggplant with a medium-sized cauliflower head cut into large florets and adjust the cooking time. The cauliflower will need to cook a bit longer and should be fork-tender, not al dente.

braised cauliflower

WITH OLIVES & CINNAMON

Long before cauliflower became the holy grail of the gluten–free, low–carb, ketogenic, and paleo set, Greeks had been cooking it in boiled salads and myriad main courses, including delicious stews. So much so that cauliflower became the bane of many a child who, coming home from school and heading straight to the kitchen, encountered the sulfurous waft and yuck factor of long–cooking cauliflower, the way traditional Greek cooks prepare it. The Greek tendency to cook cauliflower for a long time actually enhances the odor, making the smell even stronger to fresh, young nostrils. Funnily enough, the tradition of cooking it to a limpid state may be why Greeks say they "become cauliflower," meaning, they're drunk—drooping and washed out like this overcooked brassica!

But it's very healthy and versatile and no one, of course, says you have to cook it for an hour to enjoy it. Like all vegetables, cauliflower is a complex carb, but of the nonstarchy kind, with lots of fiber and little natural sugar. One cup contains about a sixth of the carbs as the same amount of pasta. It's a great source of vitamin C— a cup gives us more than half of the recommended 75 milligrams we need daily, and it provides a good amount of vitamin B6 and magnesium, as well as other B vitamins and plenty of trace minerals.

MAKES 4 SERVINGS

6 sun-dried tomatoes

⅓ cup extra-virgin Greek olive oil

1 cup chopped red onion

3 garlic cloves, finely chopped

1 medium cauliflower about 1½ to 2 pounds (680–900 g), stem trimmed and chopped and head cut into florets

1½ cups chopped plum tomatoes with juices

1 tablespoon tomato paste

½ cup dry red wine

2 bay leaves

1 cinnamon stick

1 1-inch piece orange zest, preferably from an organic orange

Greek sea salt and freshly ground black pepper to taste

16 pitted Greek green olives

2 tablespoons chopped fresh flat-leaf parsley

2 tablespoons chopped fresh parsley for garnish

Place the sun-dried tomatoes in a cup of warm water to soak for about 15 minutes, or until softened. Remove, coarsely chop, reserve the soaking water, and set aside.

Heat 3 tablespoons of olive oil in a large wide pot over medium heat and cook the onion and garlic until wilted, about 8 minutes, stirring.

Add the cauliflower pieces, toss to coat in the oil, and add the plum tomatoes and tomato paste. Add the red wine, bring to a simmer, and add the bay leaves, cinnamon, and orange zest. Add the sun-dried tomatoes. Taste the soaking liquid and, if it isn't too salty, add that to the pot as well. Season lightly with salt and pepper. Cover and simmer over low heat for about 25 minutes, or until the cauliflower is tender but still al dente. Add the olives and continue cooking for 5 minutes. Remove and serve, sprinkled with chopped fresh parsley and a little extra olive oil if desired, for garnish.

greek–style caponata

Caponata is obviously not a traditional Greek island dish! But eggplant medleys similar to this are part of the fabric of Greek cooking, and on Ikaria, there are plenty of eggplant-based main course stews. Eggplant is an important vegetable. Its meaty texture is very satisfying, and its versatility is legendary in literally everything from spreads to sweets. I often make this as an accompaniment to a very ancient Greek island recipe: fava, or puree of yellow split peas. The addition of Greek capers and caper leaves is delicious. Greek capers, especially from Santorini, which are available in the United States, have a decidedly mineral-intense flavor; their silky, briny leaves are something we love to eat, too, in cooked dishes like this and in salads.

MAKES 4 TO 6 SERVINGS

½ to ¾ cup extra-virgin
Greek olive oil

1 large red onion, chopped

2 stalks celery, diced

1 red bell pepper, diced

3 large garlic cloves, minced

1 pound (450 g) (about 8)
fresh ripe plum tomatoes,
cored and coarsely chopped

3 tablespoons coarsely
chopped pitted kalamata
or green Amfissa
or Chalkidiki olives

2 tablespoons Corinthian
currants or light or dark
raisins, preferably organic

Greek sea salt to taste

2 teaspoons *petimezi*

1 large eggplant, diced

1 tablespoon Santorini capers,
rinsed and drained

6 Santorini caper leaves,
drained and julienned

2 tablespoons toasted
pine nuts

Freshly ground pepper
to taste

2 tablespoons sweet wine
vinegar

Heat 3 tablespoons of the oil over medium heat in a large, heavy nonstick skillet, then add the onion, celery, and pepper. Cook, stirring until the onion starts to color, the pepper is soft, and the celery is lightly caramelized for about 12 to 15 minutes. Add the garlic. Cook together for a minute, until the garlic softens.

Add the tomatoes, olives, and currants or raisins. Season lightly with salt and gently stir in 2 teaspoons of *petimezi*. Cook for 15 to 20 minutes, until the mixture is thick.

Heat ½ of the remaining olive oil over medium-high heat and add about ½ of the eggplant, stirring gently until lightly browned and about halfway cooked. Remove, and set aside. Repeat with remaining eggplant. Transfer the half-cooked eggplant to the tomato mixture and toss to combine. Drizzle in the balsamic vinegar and stir. Stir in the capers, julienned caper leaves, and toasted pine nuts. Season to taste with salt and pepper. Add the sweet wine vinegar.

Cook everything together for about 6 to 7 minutes to give the ingredients and flavors a chance to meld. Remove from heat and let cool. Serve on its own as a main course, over the Heirloom Carrot Fava (page 31), pasta or rice, or even over bruschetta. It's delicious at room temperature and even better the next day!

cauliflower steak melt

WITH SPANAKOPITA

Spanakopita filling is incredibly versatile. You can use it to stuff baked sweet and regular potatoes; as a filling for omelets, grilled cheese, and lasagna; or as a low-carb version of a melt, that Greek diner classic that usually calls for open-faced tuna and American cheese! This is a great weeknight main course if you're yearning for something cheesy and indulgent without all the carbs.

As for the cauliflower itself, there's no end to the good things cauliflower offers us. High in fiber, low in carbs, and packed with nutrients, cauliflower is one of the best cruciferous vegetables we can include regularly in our diets.

MAKES 4 SERVINGS

1 large head cauliflower

4 tablespoons extra-virgin olive oil, or more as needed

Sea salt and freshly ground black pepper to taste

1 medium red onion, minced

1 shallot, minced

2 scallions, trimmed and minced

12 ounces baby spinach, rinsed and spun dry

½ cup chopped fresh dill

⅓ cup chopped fresh mint

⅓ cup chopped fresh parsley

1 clove garlic, grated

½ teaspoon freshly grated nutmeg

½ cup Greek *anthotyro* or ricotta cheese

½ cup crumbled Greek feta cheese

½ cup shredded kasseri, *graviera*, or provolone

Preheat the oven to 450°F (230°C). Line a baking sheet with parchment paper.

Remove outer leaves from cauliflower, but keep the stems intact. Set aside and chop the most tender leaves.

Place the cauliflower stem-side down on a cutting board and, using a large chef's knife, cut the cauliflower into 4 slices, each about 1 to 1½ inches thick. The 2 center slices will naturally be a little larger and contain part of the stem. Place the cauliflower slices on the prepared baking sheet. Brush both sides with half the olive oil and sprinkle with salt and pepper. Roast for about a half hour, or until tender, turning halfway through to cook and brown nicely on both sides. Remove when done and turn the oven broiler on.

Meanwhile, heat the remaining 2 tablespoons of olive oil in a large frying pan over medium-high heat. Add the onion, shallot, and scallion and cook, stirring, until translucent and soft, about 6 to 7 minutes. Stir in the garlic and then stir in the spinach, in batches if necessary, cooking it until wilted, about 5 to 6 minutes. Stir in the fresh herbs and cook for about a minute, just to wilt them. Transfer the spinach mixture to a large mixing bowl. Stir in the *anthotyro* or ricotta and feta. Season with salt, pepper, and nutmeg.

Top each cauliflower steak with about ½ cup of the spinach mixture, using a little more for the larger pieces. Spoon the grated cheese over the top of the spinach mixture and broil the cauliflower steaks until the cheese melts and starts to lightly brown, about 2 minutes. Serve immediately.

one-pot brussels sprouts & potatoes
WITH DILL & ANISE

Pretty much everything in the cabbage—*Brassica*—genus figures prominently in the local cuisine, and the original rendition of this dish calls for *papoulies*, which is very much like bok choy. I have reworked this with Brussels sprouts instead and suggest a bit of ouzo and a piece of star anise to approximate the flavor of wild fennel, which is one of the main herbs used on the island.

MAKES 4 SERVINGS

4 tablespoons extra-virgin Greek olive oil

1 cup chopped red onion

2 garlic cloves, finely chopped

8 small new potatoes, halved

Sea salt to taste

4 cups trimmed, halved Brussels sprouts

2 tablespoons ouzo or other anise-flavored liqueur (optional)

1 star anise

2 tablespoons balsamic vinegar

1 tablespoon *petimezi* (grape molasses)

Freshly ground black pepper to taste

½ to ⅔ cup vegetable stock or broth

2 tablespoons snipped fresh dill or wild fennel

1 pinch smoked salt for finishing

In a deep skillet or wide pot over medium heat, warm 2 tablespoons of olive oil and cook the onions until lightly browned. Stir in the garlic and swirl around for about ½ minute to soften.

Add the potatoes and season with salt to taste. Cover and cook until lightly browned, about 6 to 7 minutes.

Add Brussels sprouts, and stir to coat in oil. Add ouzo, if using, star anise, balsamic vinegar, and *petimezi*. Season to taste with salt and pepper. Add a half cup of the vegetable stock or broth. Cover and cook for 10 to 12 minutes, until the Brussels sprouts are al dente but tender, adding the remaining stock or broth if the mixture needs more moisture. Drizzle in the remaining olive oil, add the dill and a pinch of the smoked sea salt, and toss to combine. Serve.

vegan moussaka

In a book of recipes that emulate the spirit of plant-based Ikarian cooking, I have included a version of moussaka aimed specifically at vegans. I cooked this recipe for the vegan episode on season four of *My Greek Table*, and my daughter—and harshest critic—called it simply epic! Enjoy.

MAKES 6 TO 8 SERVINGS

2 sweet potatoes, peeled and sliced into thin ovals

Extra-virgin Greek olive oil, as needed

3 large eggplants, trimmed and sliced into long, thin ovals

Sea salt to taste

2 large red onions, chopped

4 garlic cloves, chopped

3 cups cooked black beans

1 cup canned chickpeas, keep liquid

1½ cups canned chopped tomatoes

2 tablespoons tomato paste

½ cup red wine

1 cinnamon stick

2 dried or fresh bay leaves

4 allspice berries

Dried Greek oregano to taste

1 to 2 tablespoons balsamic vinegar

2 tablespoons *petimezi*

Freshly ground black pepper to taste

FOR THE BÉCHAMEL

Leftover liquid (aquafaba) from the 15-ounce (425 g) can of chickpeas used above (see Note)

4 tablespoons extra-virgin Greek olive oil

4 scant tablespoons all-purpose flour

2 cups unsweetened coconut milk

2 cups unsweetened almond milk

Salt and white pepper to taste

Grated nutmeg to taste

½ cup bread crumbs

Place the sweet potatoes on parchment-lined baking sheets and brush them generously with olive oil. Season lightly with salt. Bake at 400°F (200°C) until softened, about 15 minutes. Remove and set aside. You can do this a day ahead.

Place the eggplants on the parchment-lined baking sheets and brush them generously with olive oil. Season lightly with salt. Bake at 400°F (200°C) until softened, about 15 minutes. Remove and set aside. You can do this a day ahead.

Make the sauce: Heat 3 tablespoons of olive oil in a large wide pot and cook the onion over medium heat until soft, lightly colored, and translucent, about 10 minutes. Stir in the garlic.

Add the drained black beans and chickpeas and stir to coat in the oil. Add the tomatoes and stir. Add the tomato paste and wine. Add the cinnamon, bay leaves, allspice berries, balsamic vinegar, and *petimezi*, and season with salt and pepper to taste. Cook the beans for 50 minutes with the cover on the pot, or until the sauce is thick and jammy.

Remove the bay leaves, allspice berries, and cinnamon. Using a slotted spoon or an immersion blender, puree about a third of the bean mixture inside the pot. Mix it well so that pureed and whole beans are combined. Adjust seasoning with additional salt, pepper, cinnamon, or allspice powder, and add the dried oregano. Set aside.

Make the vegan béchamel: Place the drained chickpea liquid (aquafaba) in the bowl of a stand mixer outfitted with a whisk attachment and whip at medium-high speed until stiff peaks form, like meringue. Set aside.

Heat the 4 tablespoons of olive oil in a large saucepan and add the flour. Stir over medium-low heat to make a roux, about 6 minutes. Add in the coconut and almond milks, while whisking, and then continue to whisk the mixture until it thickens. Season to taste with salt, pepper, and nutmeg. Cool slightly and fold in the aquafaba.

Oil the bottom of a 13 × 9-inch (33 × 22-cm) baking pan, preferably glass or ceramic. Place a sprinkling of bread crumbs on the bottom of the pan. Spread the softened potato slices in one layer. Place a layer of eggplant slices on top. Spoon the bean sauce over the eggplant layer, spreading it with a spatula or the back of a large spoon so it is evenly distributed.

Place the remaining sweet potatoes and eggplant slices in one layer. Ladle and spread the béchamel over the beans evenly and sprinkle with bread crumbs.

Place in a preheated oven at 375°F (190°C) and bake for 45 to 50 minutes, or until the béchamel is set and creamy. Remove, cool slightly, and serve.

NOTE: Aquafaba is the liquid in a can of chickpeas. It can be made by slow-cooking soaked dried chickpeas and then draining out the liquid. This starchy liquid is a great binder directly from the can and is super handy, as it whips and creates a foam. As a result, aquafaba is able to trap air, giving items structure at the same time it delivers a light crumb and lift. It's the perfect ingredient to make a fluffy vegan béchamel.

sips

OF HEALTH & WELLNESS

Healthy sips include the array of herbs that Ikarians drink and a few refreshing beverages made with yogurt or kefir, both fermented dairy products.

As for the herbs, Ikaria's famous drinking herbs number in the dozens and are one of the most important longevity-giving habits anyone, anywhere can adopt. Herbs are a key component of the Mediterranean diet as a whole, but they have a very special role, beyond perfuming food, in the folk pharmacopeia. Their therapeutic effects are common knowledge and a living tradition, passed down from one generation to the next.

On Ikaria, and in kitchens across the Mediterranean and Greece, people know to pick herbs at their peak freshness, when essential oils and aromatic properties are at their height, in spring and summer, then dry them at home, hung upside down in a shady, breezy place.

Every kitchen cupboard is a motley collection of old jars and tea tins filled with herbs. We use a few, like oregano, thyme, rosemary, and mint, as seasonings, but the vast majority, those herbs included, are made into infusions to combat a whole list of ailments. They're loaded with antioxidants: some can promote gum health and soothe stomachaches, while others combat hypertension or an oncoming cough or cold, and others can help you to fall asleep at night.

These infusions are incredibly easy to make. Just drop a teaspoon or two of dried herbs into a tea strainer, then pour on the boiling water. Steep for 10 minutes, and you're ready to go. You can add a bit of honey—it's nature's antibiotic. Herbs also make great iced tea, with a little added lemon to help quench the thirst.

Common drinking herbs and their traditional uses in Ikarian folk medicine include the following:

Chamomile. It smells faintly of green apples and blankets the island in spring with its dainty low-lying flowers. Chamomile is consumed as an aid for insomnia and is given to babies to soothe colic. It is also used topically, made into a poultice, and turned into a balm for eye inflammations and rashes. It's also a natural expectorant.

Hawthorn. Got a sore throat? Insomnia? Heart problems? Hawthorn helps with all these ailments and more, including kidney stones, dyspepsia, and diarrhea. This plant, also called *perikathe*, comes from a tree with small white flowers. It's also quite popular with the island's goats!

Mint. Ikaria has three common types of mint tea. First, there's spearmint, which is best known and mainly used in cooking; however, as a tea, it also serves as an antidote to upset stomachs. Peppermint is consumed to calm stomach cramps, menstrual pains, fevers, and colds. And last, pennyroyal, the most beloved of the mints, helps to soothe many of the same ailments as the other two mints, but it has also been used since ancient times to kickstart a woman's menstrual cycle.

Mountain Tea/Sideritis. Mountain tea is a staple in Greece, one that only grows in the mountains at very high elevations—those who pick it use the flowers, stems, and leaves of the sideritis herb. Sometimes called *tsai tou vounou* in Greek, this tea has an entire host of benefits: it helps with upset stomachs, colds, and coughs. It works as an anti-inflammatory and an excellent diuretic, and when sipped with lemon and honey, it's a good "cure" for a sore throat.

Oregano. There is certainly no dearth of recipes that call for oregano in this and countless other books that focus on the Mediterranean diet, but it's also one of the great herbal infusions. Oregano tea helps to soothe indigestion and an upset stomach and contains highly concentrated antioxidants, which fight cellular damage due to chronic disease. Oregano also has antiviral antibiotic properties, so it's just as good for your health as it is for your cooking. We also drink it when we feel a cold coming on.

Rosemary. Drink it as a salve against colds, the flu, upset stomachs, and headaches.

Sage. Greeks have revered sage since prehistoric times, as evinced in a Minoan fresco dating to 1400 BCE showing the herb being drunk. According to some studies, drinking 2 cups of sage tea each day could increase blood antioxidant levels and lower your LDL cholesterol, while also upping the "good" HDL cholesterol. It has a strong taste, so you might want to mix it with other herbs or give it a touch of sweetness with any of the amazing local honeys Greece has to offer. Ikarians make sage infusions as a way to fight colds and the flu.

Savory. A cup or two of savory tea helps our bodies to detox, and islanders drink it to soothe coughs and bronchitis. Made into poultices, it's used to soothe arthritis pain.

Other, more obscure herbs that are found, dried, and made into infusions for therapeutic use on the island are absinthe wormwood, used as a tonic; borage, for detoxing and for colds, bronchitis, and pneumonia; leaves of the chaste tree, for menstrual cramps and hormonal imbalances; elder, for colds and flu; plantain (not the banana), to disintegrate kidney stones; Saint-John's-wort, when steeped in olive oil, is used topically to heal cuts and rashes, or sipped to help stomach problems and improve mood; it's also made into an infusion to calm the stomach.

Another important category of healthy sips is fermented dairy, mainly yogurt, buttermilk, and kefir. All have been revered in the Eastern Mediterranean for eons.

Greek Yogurt. Greek yogurt is many things, depending on where you are. What we know as Greek yogurt in the United States is made with cow's milk and—one hopes—strained (as opposed to thickened with the likes of guar gum or other coagulants), creating a creamy, protein-rich yogurt that has become one of the bestselling products of all time.

What we know as Greek yogurt in the States is called *straggisto*, or strained yogurt, in Greece. In Greece, besides strained yogurt, there are many other types, all of them delicious, made with cow's milk, sheep's milk, or goat's milk.

Buttermilk. Buttermilk is traditionally made with the leftover liquid after churning milk into butter. Greeks call it *xynogala*. Today, though, most buttermilk is cultured. It is a combination of water, lactose, and casein (milk protein) to which lactic acid–producing cultures have been added. Those cultures give buttermilk its sour taste and extend its shelf life. It's thicker than milk and very versatile and is often used in baking, but it makes a very refreshing summer quaff, especially when blended with fresh fruit and chilled.

Kefir. Kefir, fizzy, fermented, and tangy, is sometimes called the champagne of milk. Kefir is a fermented milk product similar to yogurt, with its origins in the Caucasus Mountains. Bacteria and yeast are both used to ferment kefir. Its light, foamy but creamy texture makes it perfect for smoothies and other. It is enjoyed all over the Eastern Mediterranean as a nutritious summer cooler.

sparkling mint & citrus iced tea

Tea, especially herbal tea, is one of the seminal ingredients in the Ikarian longevity diet. Many herbal teas contain specific therapeutic benefits and are diuretic, which means they help combat hypertension. But black tea such as Earl Grey also has its benefits. Black tea can aid heart health and diabetes and is high in antioxidants, among other benefits. And, having a pitcher of delicious iced tea on hand is reason to invite over a friend and celebrate the simple pleasures of life, another secret to living long and well.

Always store your iced tea in a glass pitcher or Mason jar and not in plastic or metal containers. Plastic absorbs and releases flavors, while metal will definitely impart a tinny, metallic taste, especially pronounced with black teas, which are tannic.

FOR 1½ QUARTS

2 green tea bags

2 Earl Grey tea bags

2 tablespoons dried mint, preferably Greek

2 cups boiling water

2 medium oranges

1 medium lemon

2 cups fresh orange juice

¼ cup fresh lemon juice

3 tablespoons Greek honey

750 ml seltzer, chilled

Ice cubes

Additional fresh mint for garnish (optional)

Place tea bags and dried mint in a teapot and add boiling water. Cover and steep for 5 minutes. Strain the tea into a pitcher.

Peel and section 2 oranges and 1 lemon and add to the pitcher. Stir in the orange juice, lemon juice, and honey. Cover and refrigerate for 2 hours or up to 8.

Just before serving, strain and discard the fruit from tea. Stir in the seltzer. Serve over ice, garnished with additional fresh mint if desired.

iced herbal tea

WITH FRESH PEACHES

MAKES 6 CUPS

1 heaping teaspoon
dried sage

2 heaping teaspoons
dried mint

1 heaping teaspoon
chamomile

½ cup fresh lemon verbena
leaves or 1 tablespoon dried

Honey, if desired

4 firm, ripe peaches, peeled
or unpeeled, as desired,
pitted, and sliced into wedges

1 cup ice, plus more,
for serving

1 tablespoon fresh lemon
juice, plus more if desired

Fresh peach slices, for serving

Fresh mint, for serving

Bring 4 cups of water to a boil, remove from the heat, and add the loose herbs. Allow the tea to steep for 10 minutes. If you want to sweeten it, add the honey while the tea is warm so that it dissolves better. Let the tea cool to room temperature.

Place the peaches and ice in a large pitcher. Pour in the cooled tea and lemon juice and swirl around to combine. Chill for at least 2 hours, and serve directly from the fridge over ice, with additional peach slices and fresh mint for garnish, if desired.

roasted apple–tahini smoothie
WITH CINNAMON & SESAME SEEDS

Thirst-quenching fruit purees and sippable fermented dairy drinks have been a part of the Mediterranean landscape for centuries, if not millennia. But it wasn't until the twentieth century came along that the smoothie was born, alongside the refrigerator and the blender for home use, in the 1930s.

I chose to make this smoothie vegan and call it a healthy snack or quick meal option. You can cheat and use Greek (or other) honey, preferably raw, in place of maple syrup. It does call for a little sugar, in addition to calcium-packed tahini and sesame seeds; brown sugar, surprisingly, is also a rich source of calcium and potassium.

MAKES 2 TO 4 SERVINGS

4 apples of choice (Granny Smith, Fuji, or McIntosh), peeled, cored, and cut into 1-inch (2½-cm) chunks

1 scant teaspoon cinnamon

1 pinch sea salt

1 cup unsweetened coconut or almond milk

3 tablespoons tahini

2 tablespoons chopped fresh mint

1 tablespoon Greek honey, or maple syrup if you want to make this vegan

1 cup ice cubes

1 to 2 scant teaspoons toasted sesame seeds

Preheat oven to 400°F (200°C). Toss the apple chunks with cinnamon and a pinch of salt on a parchment-lined rimmed baking sheet and bake for about 15 minutes, or until the chunks are soft and juicy, tossing about halfway through.

Transfer three-quarters of the apples to a blender. Add the coconut or almond milk, tahini, mint, honey, and 1 cup of ice cubes. Pulse until smooth. Using a metal spoon, smash the remaining apples to a jammy consistency in a bowl with a fork.

Divide smoothies among 2 or 4 glasses and top with a little of the jammy mashed apples and sesame seeds.

pear, yogurt & oat smoothie

My adult children enlightened me on the virtues of both nut butters (beyond the peanut butter that made it into their lunch sandwiches and made them the object of much curiosity in Greek public elementary schools!) and nondairy milks from oats, almond, and coconut (more likable to our Mediterranean palates than soy milk). This smoothie is really a meal in liquid form, very filling and super quick to make. Enjoy it for breakfast, lunch, or a snack.

Freezing the pears overnight reduces the amount of ice needed for blending the next day and results in a thick and creamy texture.

MAKES 2 SERVINGS

3 large pears, such as Red Anjou, peeled, seeded, and chopped

1¾ cups almond, coconut, or oat milk

1 cup Greek yogurt

⅔ cup quick-cooking oats

1 to 3 tablespoons maple syrup or Greek honey, as desired

2 tablespoons almond butter

1¼ teaspoons finely grated fresh ginger

⅛ teaspoon ground cinnamon, plus more for garnish

1 pinch coarse sea salt

6 to 12 ice cubes, or as needed

Freeze pears in a single layer on a baking sheet overnight.

Combine pears, milk, yogurt, oats, ice, maple syrup or honey, almond butter, ginger, cinnamon, and a pinch of salt in a blender and process on high speed until smooth. Add the ice cubes and continue blending at high speed.

Blend on low speed, then gradually increase speed to high. Blend until smooth, 1 to 2 minutes. Pour into chilled glasses, and garnish with ground cinnamon. Serve immediately.

kefir smoothie

WITH NECTARINES & APRICOTS

Picture this: A summer day. A lazy mom. A hungry teenage boy. Beach time beckoning. Smoothies like this one are healthy, fast, and filling, the perfect example of the Mediterranean diet on the go! It helps to have a few apricot trees and a nectarine or peach tree in the garden, but even if you don't, look for ripe fruit at peak season for the best flavor!

MAKES 2 TO 4 SERVINGS

8 ice cubes

2 cups chilled kefir

3 large ripe unpeeled apricots, pitted and chopped

2 ripe unpeeled nectarines, pitted and chopped

1 tablespoon Greek pine or blossom honey, or more as desired

1 pinch cinnamon powder

Ice water as needed

Mint sprigs for garnish

Puree everything together in a blender at high speed. Add a little ice water if needed to thin out the smoothie to desired consistency and serve immediately, garnished with a mint sprig or two and a dusting of cinnamon powder.

acknowledgments

As always, I have a lot of people to thank for helping to bring this book together.

To all my Ikaria cooking school guests past and future, I am more than grateful, and I learn as much from you as you do, I hope, from our unique little patch of paradise. This book, indeed, was inspired by the exchange of ideas around my kitchen counter during one such week a few years ago. I owe a special debt of gratitude to three guests, Marta Adelman, Raelene Fulford, and Amy Gold, who graciously allowed me to use many of their photos from our week together on Ikaria.

Thank you to Lizana Mitropoulou, Lida Papamatthaiaki, and Chryssa Sereli, our Ikaria class dream team, who have become friends and work together so well, making everyone's experience seamless, happy, delicious, and most memorable! Thank you to Carolina Doriti, friend, kindred spirit, and colleague, whose food sense is so well-honed and whose styling graces these pages. And to Lida, again, for cooking and helping with the photography, too! It's hard to find words for Vasilis Stenos, a gifted Renaissance man, twin soul, family, and friend. His aesthetics have informed every part of my life, and his photographs the pages of this book. Thank you.

Michael Flamini, my editor, lent his sharpened pencil and sharp eye to the manuscript, but mostly he supported the idea for this book and encouraged the next one, still to come! A great copyeditor is a blessing for every writer, no matter her subject, and I was saved more than a few times by the watchful eye of Julia DeGraf. Heartfelt thanks to Janis Donnaud, my agent, at the ready to go to bat, shape an idea, and help create the best book possible.

And, last but not least, to my family: My beautiful sisters, Athena and Koko, and their extended clans and, of course, my own kids, Kyveli and Yiorgo. You're the greatest blessing of all.

index

about the author

DIANE KOCHILAS, celebrity chef, award-winning cookbook author, and cooking school owner, has been at the forefront of bringing healthy, delicious Greek cuisine to a wide international audience for many years. She is the host and co-executive producer of *My Greek Table*, a thirteen-part cooking-travel series about Greece and Greek cuisine airing nationally on public television. She runs the Glorious Greek Cooking School on her native island, Ikaria.